The Same and Yet So Different

The Same and Yet So Different

You Can't Run from Who You Are

LESIA LIPZ

Order this book online at www.trafford.com
or email orders@trafford.com

Most Trafford titles are also available at major online book retailers.

Printed in the United States of America.

ISBN: 978-1-4907-3749-2 (sc)
ISBN: 978-1-4907-3750-8 (hc)
ISBN: 978-1-4907-3751-5 (e)

Library of Congress Control Number: 2014909740

Trafford rev. 05/29/2014

www.trafford.com
North America & international
toll-free: 1 888 232 4444 (USA & Canada)
fax: 812 355 4082

I dedicate this book in loving memory of my mama Sandra Franklin also Loniel Franklin, Latonia Franklin, Francis Crain, Lori Reese, Larry Quinney, Aunt Ruth & Uncle Howard Lenton.

I would like to give acknowledgments to my husband Leon, my mother-in-law Mildred Blankenship; my brother Loniel (Tony) Franklin; Melvine Perry; Adonia & Henry Flakes; Tiffany & Mitch Joyner; Delshawn Foster my god-brother; my children Jamell & Latesia Franklin; Jeffrey Perry Jr.; Ramon & Terrick Jr. Griffin; Tamisha, Diamond, and Whitney Rush; Ciera, Brianne, and Lil Leon Blankenship; Kenneth & Marissa; Allen Shepard; Deanna & Dashane my goddaughters; my grandchildren; Ta'Niiya Taylor; Jayla and Ryan Perry; Serenity and Alana Franklin; JaLon Hollen; Shanay, Danial & Lauren for bearing my grandchildren ;Francine & Shawnta Shorts; Courtnay Clay; Darlena Harvey; Laverta Baker; Patrice Mitchell; Angel Ewings—Gooden; Ladone Boyd; Dorrinda Franklin; and Aunt Faustina for being supportive at times when I really needed you all. Jeffrey Perry Sr., Terrick Griffin Sr., and Allen Colbert Jr.—thank you all for being the best fathers ever. All my nephews, nieces, aunts, uncles & cousins. The Perkins Family; The Franklin Family; The Crain Family; The Bridgewater Family; The Shorts Family, The Jackson Family,

The Corbin Family; The Perry Family, The Griffin Family, The Colbert Family, Friends & Associates. Also to the people who motivated me to continue writing after reading only a few pages. You all mean so much to me.

Luv

Women I Can Count On

Growing up and not being able to completely trust women like my mother, grandmother, aunts, sisters, daughters, or girlfriends put a huge strain on my life after being let down by so many of them. Saying you are a friend of mine as an adult was something that had to be proven to me. My sister Tonia was the only person that I felt was my true friend, and she felt exactly the same way about the females that were in her circle.

I was blessed by God when I came into contact with a young lady when I was twenty-seven years old. She was named Darlena Cook, and she lived in Port Huron, Michigan. Dar-Dar is what I called her. She was a true breath of fresh air. From the moment we were introduced, we clicked. From the jump, she was genuinely true to her heart. We were introduced by our men. They became friends while they were serving time in prison. Dar has never let me down or changed. She is a woman of her word and is always the first person that I call when I need an honest opinion. Dar has seen all my children grow from children to adults. It has now been twenty plus years, and we're still the best of friends and are always there for one another when needed.

Then there is Laverta Baker. I call her Byrd. She was a young lady that I didn't meet until I was thirty-nine years old. We were coworkers that only saw each other in passing to transfer documents from one department to another. Until one day, she overheard me telling one of my other coworkers that I had worked with for over four years that I would be quitting my job there soon, because my car had broken down and I had no way back and forth to work from the city to the suburban area. She immediately interrupted the conversation and asked me, "Where do you live?" I told her, and she said without hesitation, "I can pick you up and take you home. My daughter goes to school not far from where you live." This shocked the hell out of me.

She barely even knew me. I quickly accepted the offer with pay, that she refused but, I would sneak and put in different places around her car so she would take it. Gas was not for free and I appreciated her to the fullest. We have been friends for eight years now. She showed me that there are still some good people left in the world.

I love these two women; until death do our friendships part. Friendship is just like a marriage. You have to work at it for it to last.

My sister/cousin Patrice—she has been by my side since the days I began writing my daily experiences about my life. Trecia is what I call her she is the person who hears me out no matter what and values my opinion about life. She is also the first person who made me become fully aware of certain things about myself that needed to be worked on. I know without a doubt that she has my back no matter right or wrong she has become a strong willed hard working woman and gives me credit for a lot of that. I only tried to do for you what Melvine did for me. Be there. I love you cousin and I am so proud of you. I can say you did it. You paid attention. ☺

Now, there is Dorrinda—my sister-in-law, but I call her Dirty Diana and it took a long time before we finally clicked. It was because I had given my friendship to all the women my brother was ever in a relationship with in the past, but once the relationship ended, they all turned on me as if it were my fault that it didn't work out. One thing about me as a woman is that if I had a friendship with the family of whomever I was in a relationship with, it never changed because we were no longer together. I look at this as being childish or an untrue person.

So because of this, I gave Dorrinda a very hard time no matter how nice she was to me, but in the end she was there for me on more than one occasion and at times I least expected her to be.

For instance, when I was in the hospital, she volunteered to bathe me because I could not do it for myself. Also, whenever my legs began weaken due to my illness, she is usually the first to notice. I have heard her whispering to my brother, "Look, Tony, her leg is dragging." So I prayed on it. I asked God if it was okay for me to open up to her. Please show me, Lord. Then one day, he revealed to me that she was a true friend indeed. From that day forward, I can say I am happy to have her as my sister-in-law.

Of course, my big sister Melvine the one who gave me the best advice of all the women I have ever encountered. I will forever be in her debt. She is the strongest woman I know. We still talk and see one another on occasions but it doesn't matter how much time comes between us. We bounce right back as if we have never been out of touch. I love you from the bottom of my heart Sister and thank god for putting you in my Life. I am a product of you girl. Great Job!

There is one more person that I must mention. She is one of my oldest friends who is no longer here with us that I looked at more like a sister than a friend. Her name was Lori Reese. We became friends when we were in high school. We went through a whole lot together—some good, some bad. Lori was the person that kept me in prayer she did all she could to help me become a born again Christian. We joined the same church twice, we song in the choir together. She wanted me to be on the right side of the Lord, is what she use to tell me. Lori was the person that you could count on to be present. Half of my family didn't know she wasn't a blood related family member. Lori was guaranteed to be present to all events because was a devoted friend. Not perfect by far, but who really is. It took her not being here for me to realize how much our friendship really meant to me. Lori passed away in 2010. She had a brain tumor for many years and suffered from complications during surgery when she decided to have it removed. Since her passing, I have taken my life much more seriously, and being happy has become my top priority. We only live once, and it is all we get.

My new motto is: Effective immediately that we should show the ones we love that we love them while they are still breathing because we never know the day life will end for any of us.

I love and miss you, Lori Ann Reese, my sister from another mother!

I forgive you Lori. I just wish I wasn't so stubborn then, so I could have told you before now. ☹

My Mama

It was the spring of 1973. I was only six years old. My mother Sandra, father Loniel, sister Tonia, brother Tony, and I were all living on the northwest side of Detroit. My mama was a twenty-six-year-old married woman to my father Loniel. She worked at a well-known health insurance company for several years and could type her ass off, and she typed approximately 120 wpm. She complained all the time about how tired she was of her job, but I always thought it had a lot to do with her not having a strong enough man in her corner to provide support and assist with her success.

Mama graduated with honors at the age of sixteen, then she went straight to business school to become an executive secretary. She got married very young at eighteen years old and, on top of that, married a man that she did not really love. She married him only because she was five and a half months pregnant with my older sister, Tonia. Even though my father knew the baby wasn't his, he loved her so much that it didn't matter. One thing for sure, we never noticed any differences regarding the way Daddy treated us. It was always equally balanced. As I got older, Mama told me that she grew to love my father over time. Because of that reason alone, she said he was a real man.

Their marriage only lasted nine years before they separated. My sister's real father, Larry, was on his way home from prison. Once Mama found out, she wanted him back in her life. He resurfaced about a year after my father moved out. It wasn't long before he was living in the house with us. Mama was a very slim woman, about 5'5", golden-brown complexion, sandy-brown hair, brown eyes, and she had a bold attitude. She would say whatever came to mind without any worry as to what a person felt about it. She was a small-built woman who could hold her own. She was loved by everyone. She loved to smile, party, and just have a good time.

I saw a much happier person in her after Daddy left. She was not as uptight. With Larry, she wasn't smoking as many cigarettes or drinking as many beers. Mama cooked more often and did not go straight to her bedroom once she came home from work like she used to do when she was with Daddy. We even did more family events together, like going to the Christmas carnivals, out to dinner, and to the movies. Mama even tried to learn how to drive, which did not go so well. She drove right through our elementary school fence and on to the playground and never attempted driving again after that.

All Mama wanted out of life was to be happy and live a stress-free life with a man who knew what the title of being a man was—respecting, trusting, and providing unconditional love to his woman. She knew what it took to get a man. It was just that her choice of men was always wrong in the end. Mama had drug addicts, jailbirds, working men who didn't want to be in a relationship, or another woman's man. Then there's Daddy who genuinely loved her to death, but he could not control his emotions. He was so damn jealous that he beat her to try and control her, so this is what caused him to lose her in the long run.

Living in this house was a trip. Our landlord lived above us. The homeowner was about sixty-five years old. When we moved there, she was a very mean and grouchy old lady. From the day we moved in, there were problems daily, but overall we had some good memories living there also. Since my brother and I had birthdays in the winter months, we celebrated with my sister. Every August, she had a big party in the backyard. We also had a cool tree house that we would all hang out in. There was this abandoned building that we would all go inside to explore. Growing up in this area was not all that bad. There was not as much crime, plus the neighbors all got along like family.

Mama would give herself a house birthday party every year. She would put in colored lightbulbs throughout the house, a red bulb in the den where they smoked weed, a blue bulb in the dining room where they danced, a yellow bulb in the bathroom so they could see the toilet seat, and she pushed the dining room table in the corner to make space for them to dance.

The menu was tuna salad and crackers, fried chicken, a baked birthday cake, plus plenty of beer, wine, and liquor.

We had to eat dinner early, take our baths, and use the toilet before the party started. We had to go to bed, and we better not come out of the bedroom for anything at all. We had to stay in our bedrooms until the music stopped. This was usually not until about five the next morning. Mama would tell us to try her and we were going to get our ass whipped. I never liked getting whippings, so I did just what I was told and took my black behind to sleep.

What I loved most about Mama was watching her get ready for work in the morning. She was so classy with her preparations. She would get out of the shower with her Noxzema on her face, then sit at her vanity mirror and remove it with care, then she would put moisturizer on her entire body with ease. She wore a fragrance called Charisma that smelled awesome. She would then slip on her pantyhose so elegantly. Her suits were top of the line, and her heels were too. She was a 100 percent businesswoman just like I wanted to become when I grew up.

Mama would lay out our clothes for school and put our breakfast on the stove if she had enough time to cook us a hot meal. If not, she would wake us up before she walked out of the door, letting us know what we could eat for breakfast. Off to the bus stop, headed downtown to work every day, she had to leave home at 6:00 a.m. to arrive by 8:00 a.m. This meant my siblings and I were responsible for dressing ourselves, eating breakfast, and getting to school. Our school was only one block over from our home. Mama would get home around six every night and prepare dinner for us. She taught my sister and me to do laundry and clean the house to cut down all the household work being put on herself, and we both looked after our younger brother, Tony.

Being a single mother of three young children was not an easy job, but Mama pulled it off. She paid her bills on time, kept a job and a roof over our head, and took good care of us. We had what we needed, not always what we wanted. Most of all, Mama always had a man in her life.

She wasn't perfect, but I will always love my mama.

My Daddy

Loniel Franklin was his government name. He stood about 5'8" with a dark complexion, medium build, cold black nice-textured hair, and a pink-black lower lip. He was known as Pink Lips even though only one of them was pink. He worked several good-paying jobs for the city from being a garbage man to a foreman at Ford Motor Company. Even though they were separated, he stopped by the house every payday to give Mama some money, also to check on us. He tried time and time again to get back with Mama after the breakup, but she was done with him. He wasn't giving up that easy. He loved his wife and children. He could not believe it was really over.

The first Christmas after he moved out was the best one ever. Daddy went all out for us, trying to impress Mama, but she still told him they were not going to get back together. So one evening, after the New Year, Mama went out with her girls. We were being kept by our babysitter from next door. My dad came through one of the living room windows and stole the TV and stereo set that he had gotten us for Christmas back. The sitter saw him come in and leave, but she was so afraid she just laid there and played sleep. She let my mother know what happened later, and you know, he denied it all. Now Daddy was not allowed inside our house at all anymore. When he came for a visit, we had to go outside and talk to him in his car in front of the house.

After about a year, Daddy got serious with this woman, and they moved in together. She had three children around our ages. My parents decided it was time for us to go visit on one weekend. She turned out to be a nice lady and so were her kids. We all got along well over that weekend, then we began asking to go visit almost every weekend thereafter. This turned into entire summer visits.

This went on for about five more years. Then one day, my mother received a call from my daddy's girlfriend stating she should keep my sister and me away from Daddy because he had raped her daughter. We knew this was a lie. My daddy was a lot of things but *not a rapist.* This woman pressed charges against my daddy, and he went to jail for months before the truth finally came out, and he was released from jail. The jury dismissed the case because her daughter slipped up on cross-examination and admitted that her own father told her to make all the lies up all along.

We were entering our teenage years before my daddy got into another relationship, but this time, he made sure the woman did not have any daughters. This woman had two sons, so now my brother finally got a chance to spend time with our old man. I was happy for Tony because it meant a lot to him too to spend time with Daddy. Sometimes Tonia and I would go also just to visit our grandma and granddaddy or to hang out with Daddy going fishing or a cookout with his friends. I saw a whole lot during my visits with Daddy (things I should not have seen at such a young age).

When we would go fishing with Daddy, he would get so drunk. Because fishing was an all-day thing for us, we're up bright and early by 4:00 a.m., carrying out coolers, fishing poles, blankets, folding chairs, and most importantly, the big picnic basket full of all my favorite fisherman food. Daddy would eat sardines, Vienna sausages, liver cheese or pottage meat, and crackers with his beer or liquor, always vodka or gin. These were times to remember.

Whenever Daddy would drink, he gave us whatever we asked for. Ice cream from the truck, chips, candy, and all the pop we wanted to drink. It would first start off super fun. Everyone would be talking, laughing, and singing, then to the arguing, fussing, and fighting, then a very long and scary ride back to their house, and all I did was pray the whole way back. It was always that way. But for some reason, this didn't stop me from wanting to keep going back over to my daddy's house.

There is nothing like the love a little girl has in her heart for her daddy.

LARRY, MY SISTER'S FATHER

Larry was a very handsome man. He stood about 5'7", somewhat on the chubby side, with very fine brown curly hair. He had hair only around the side and back, and he was bald on top, so he wore a hat most of the time. What I like about Larry most was that when he was around, Mama always smiled, so I knew she was happy, and this made me happy too.

Larry was home with us during the day whenever there was no school and always gone at night. Once Mama got home and settled in, he would be out the door after about an hour or so. Downtown is where he said he was headed every day. At the time, I had no idea that this is where most of the drug addicts hung out. Every night, upon his return, he would wake us in the middle of the night with either some banana pudding or peach cobbler.

All us kids thought he worked at a bakery or a restaurant but later found out very different. He sold drugs and used drugs while he was away, and after a year or so, I began to see a change in him. He would be very sluggish and appeared sleepy a lot. I later would catch him nodding off. His head would be bobbing and weaving, eyes closed, and his mouth slightly open. Not really aware of what was going on in his surroundings but could finish a conversation all at the same time.

This shit was weird and funny, my first encounter of a heroin addict. No matter what, I loved him in just this short period of time because he was a good person and a good man, just not good to himself. I wondered what happened in his life to start his using drugs. Or did it begin while he was in prison? I dare not ask. I knew I would be smacked in the mouth for even forming my lips to ask a question like that. So I came up with my own reasons in my mind, and it made me feel sorry for him.

Larry got a job working security for a historical site close to downtown on the midnight shift. One night on his day off, he was watching us while Mama went out with her girlfriends.

He was called in to work, so we had to go with him. I had the time of my life in this very old and big mansion that belonged to the rich woman the site was named after. She lived there until her passing away. It had a beautiful grandfather clock in the living room of the house that dinged on the hour. I enjoyed the sound of the dinging.

I realized I loved large spaces and dreamed of having a large home of my own one day. I was so comfortable in this place. Larry gave us a tour of the mansion during his patrols. The home had a cafeteria for the kitchen. The bedrooms were the size of three rooms in our house. The bathroom was so pretty; it was fit for a queen. He put us all to bed in one of the rooms together, and he sat beside the bed as we slept. That was special to me—the time he spent with us. I'm not sure if my sister or brother thought of it as big of a deal as I did.

I kept that memory with me until the day Larry died. Because he could have just dropped us off at our granny's house, but he spent some quality time with us and I noticed.

One night, around 3:00 a.m., I heard a loud noise. It was my mama screaming, "What happened? What happened? Just bring him home." Before long there was a knock at the door, and a gang of men I never saw before carried Larry in the house to my mother's room. Blood was everywhere. Larry was yelling, "San, call the doctor now!" She got the phone, called someone, and said it was going to be a minute. Next thing I remember, there was another knock at the door, and a man in all black walked in. He was so dark I couldn't see his eyes.

He went to my mama's bedroom with two of the men that brought him home and slammed the door. Within minutes, Larry was crying out so loud my body cringed. I put my hands over my ears. I couldn't stand it. This went on for over thirty minutes before it was complete silence. I knew Larry was dead. The door opened, and the men all left. No one said a word. They walked out the front door and never looked back. I waited and knew nothing until the following morning. Larry was okay. I believe he was given some very strong drugs to allow him to sleep by the street doctor.

It was months after before I overheard a conversation by the adults that I was not supposed to hear. They were saying that Larry could have died from the gunshot to his leg. It will never be the same ever again. Once Larry recovered, he had a slight limp on his right side. I would French braid his hair on every other Friday when he got paid so I could buy a few things for myself. Tonia would act like he was invisible. She wondered why he was living with us, where he came from, and hoped he went back wherever he came from.

Just before Tonia's eleventh birthday, my granny was drunk and came to our house to tell her that Larry was her natural father in front of all our friends. From that day forward, my sister was a changed person.

Tonia no longer performed well in school. She despised his presence. She told him she hated him every chance she got. This really hurt Larry—to know his oldest child felt this way about him. He tried everything he could to show her how sorry he was for not being in her life all along. But she just said, “Loniel is my daddy, not you.” Larry finally gave up on trying and just figured time would heal it all, but that never happened.

When push came to shove, Larry was not my father, but I loved him as if he were.

Young and Not So Innocent

It was the summer of 1977. I remember it like yesterday. This was the best summer of my life when I was a kid. We spent it in Pontiac, Michigan, at our aunt and uncle's house. We loved it up there. It was like going to another state, but it was less than an hour away from where we lived. Up there, a kid could be a kid. We felt safe and free. We played kickball in the middle of the street and baseball in the backyards that were all open fields no fences, and most of all, we could stay outside after midnight. Boy, did we love it there.

I was just a few months shy of my eleventh birthday and beginning to feel like a young woman faster than anyone could ever imagine. I was a little too much to handle as the older people would say; that's just another way of them saying I was hot in the ass. To be perfectly honest with you, I was. You see, I liked boys, and I liked them a lot, much more than I should have at that age. I always felt that I had been touched inappropriately by someone, and it caused me to become very promiscuous. But whoever it was must have been very close to me that I blocked the memory out.

Summer was coming to an end quickly. I started my period for the first time, and Mama said it was time to come back to our new home. We met some friends during our stay, four cute brothers that just happened to live on the same street as we did in Detroit. Once I met one of their friends named Leon, it was love at first sight. From the time I met him, I woke up early and tried to stay outside as long as I could before Mama yelled our names to get inside for the night. Before that summer was over, I experienced all my first times with him. He taught me how to kiss and how good it felt to have my private rubbed or getting my nipples sucked. I also had my first full sexual encounter with him. Leon was very persuasive. He could have talked me into doing almost anything during this time.

Sad to say but it did not last for very long before Leon was running behind another girl. Also, I went through my first little heartbreak with Leon. I liked him so much that I just went anywhere to be with him even in his garage on the ground and let him have his way with me. No matter how bad Leon treated me, whenever I saw him, I could not resist him. We still had sex for the next two years. All he had to do was call me, and I was there. I knew Leon was just using me, but he made me feel good when we were together. Even if it was only for five minutes. Leon was an only child of his mother, and he was the most spoiled person I ever knew. Things had to be his way or no way at all. His stubbornness is what I think I liked about him the most.

This was my first time loving someone more than they loved me.

I liked living in this new neighborhood. It was more of an upper middle-class area in the early eighties before it began to change slowly but surely. We lived with my uncle and his wife in the downstairs two-family unit, with my cousins and their mother living upstairs, which were my uncle's children and their mother.

It took me some time before I was able to figure all that out too. I used to hang out with all the boys. They were my friends. There were six of us—five boys and one girl. At all times, they took care of me and made sure nobody bothered me. As I know you're aware, this made all the females in the hood have a certain dislike for me just because I had five of the finest guys in the hood hanging out with me. I didn't care. I never liked being around girls anyway, so "oh well" is how I felt about it.

We used to ride the yellow bus to school every day. We attended Vetal Middle School. The school was at least five miles away from where we lived. My best friend was a bully because he was the tallest of us all, so he thought he was the leader of our pack. He used to sit next to me on the bus for two years straight in the same seat. We had no assigned seats, so we could have sat anywhere we wanted. He was out sick for a full week with the flu, and Leon sat with me on the bus. Someone told him when he returned to school the following Monday while we waited for the bus to pull up. Once the bus got there and parked. He asked me if it was true that Leon sat in his seat when he was sick.

I told him, "Yes, he did." Before I could blink, he pushed me down so hard that I flew under the bus right through a puddle of slushy ice water. I got up and ran all the way home. I was so embarrassed.

I beat on the front door as hard as I could before my aunt opened the door, wanting to know what just happened to me. I was in tears and so hurt by this. I didn't know what to do. She called my mother at work to let her know about the incident. She left work early to come home. She was furious. She never liked my best friend from the start. She thought he was a smart-ass from the first time she saw him. "What's his home number?" she asked. I called it out to her.

His mother answered. They talked for a while in private. Then she came out of her bedroom and told me to put my coat and boots on, and before long, we were at Vetal picking him up from school. Once we got back to our block, they both beat his ass with a belt. Mama and I walked back down the street to our house. He never bullied me again after that. He even allowed me to do things to him that no other girl could without getting punched.

This was the first time a guy ever displayed jealousy over me.

Also the first time a boy fought for me. Rumor had it that Leon took up for me. He and Shawn had a few words back and forth that almost lead to a fight over me.

It was eighth-grade graduation morning, the day before Father's Day. Larry asked what I wanted for graduation since he could not attend. I told him to surprise me. Bright and early the next day, the phone rang, and my mother was screaming. "No! No! Who is this?" We later found out that the call was about Larry. He was found dead downtown in a motel room. The details of his death still remain a mystery.

During the funeral, who walked in much to my surprise? My daddy. He took two buses to get to this funeral. Once he saw me, he walked over and kissed me and Tonia on the cheek, hugged Tony, and sat down beside me for a while. The service started. The music was playing, and a lady was singing a sad song. I began to cry.

My daddy grabbed my face in his hand and looked me in my eyes and told me, "You better wipe those tears right now, that's not your daddy. What the hell you crying for goddamn it?" I was furious with him for that statement, but I kept it to myself. I believe I never looked at my daddy the same after that day.

The loss of Larry destroyed my mother and pretty much our family. Mama started dating all kinds of stray-ass niggas. We ended up moving with my granny, my mother's mom. Wow! Have you ever heard the term "from sugar to shit"? Well, if you haven't, you're about to learn what it means.

Granny's House

My granny was a very attractive woman. The kind of woman that most black men wanted back in the forties and fifties. Granny was so pretty that she even knew it. She had a very light complexion, with gray eyes, and coarse sandy-brown hair, which she hated because it was the only thing that reminded her that she was really a black woman. Her mother was black, but her father was a mixed man who looked white. More than likely, his father was a white man and his mother was black. I never got the chance to meet him, but my granny told me all about him. Being a lighter woman really helped my granny get by in her day. Whites were nicer to her, but blacks were mean to her. So this made her develop a certain hatred toward darker people.

Granny as I knew her was somewhat of a stern person. She didn't smile much at all and always seemed to give me a hard time no matter what I did. I was not good enough in her eyes. As a child, I was the one of at least four granddaughters who had to wash all the dishes on the holidays. Or was given whatever chore everyone else didn't want to do. Over the years, my mother along with my aunts and uncles all felt that I was just lazy and just never wanted to clean at all. But that wasn't it. Granny made me feel like an outcast every chance she got. This caused me to grow to hate her for many years plus have a problem against all light-skinned people.

Granny was a gambler, also a loan shark in her neighborhood, and I'm sure she had many enemies that she was not aware of due to this. Parties went on all the time at her house until the wee hours of the morning. Gallons of vodka or gin would be on the table, there was loud music, and people argued over one thing or another at the gambling parties. Crackheads were in and out at all times of the day and night trying to sell or pawn one thing or another to my granny to get a piece of crack or some heroin.

Most children looked forward to a visit at Grandmother's house but not me. I hated to see the weekends coming.

Just the possibility of it made me sick to my stomach. What could I do about it? Nothing! I was a child who had to deal with it up until I was ten years old. This was when I decided to talk to my mother about the way I felt about Granny. I explained that I didn't feel she liked me at all or that she really didn't want me to come to her house. So I asked my mother to just pay close attention to how Granny treats me when we're at her house. Mama agreed to do this for me. Finally, the weekend approached, and we were home from school and on our way to Granny's house. I was so happy to go for the first time since I was five years old.

We entered the house. It's full of alcoholics, gamblers, and crackheads as usual. Granny immediately said to me, "Take your black ass upstairs now." I looked at Mama. I went upstairs. Not long after, she called for me to come down and told me to fix a pot of smoked sausages for her guest. I took care of it. I made all their plates then returned upstairs. After about an hour or so, Granny called me once more and told me to pick up everyone's plates and wash them.

Mama said, "Why does she have to wash them? Tonia is upstairs also."

Granny said, "Because I told her to do them."

Mama said, "She just cooked the sausages and made the plates."

Granny said, "So fucking what!"

Mama then told me to go upstairs and tell my sister Tonia to come down to wash the dishes. All hell broke loose. They argued back and forth until Mama told us to get our things; it was time to go. That was my last visit to my granny's house for over two years. Then what do you know, we had to go live there for a few months.

Well, as you all know, I was about to turn twelve years old now. I had started my menstrual cycle a little over a year ago and was feeling like a young woman. I was able to express myself much better. Going there was like the movie Flowers in the attic.

I woke up, went to school, came home, did my chores, stayed clear of Granny, went back to the attic where we sleep, and started all over the next day.

Winter was coming fast. A van full of teenagers posted up and began selling drugs from the driveway between the house next door and Granny's house.

There was one guy that was a worker that I found to be attractive, and I believed he like me also. I found out later that he only talked to me to find out what my sister's name was. This was fine because I knew she had eyes for the oldest guy of the group. So there were no worries for me about them getting together. I walked to the store at least twice before darkness came every day. The guys would pay me to bring them things back from the store for them. This became a side hustle for me to make a little money daily. They paid me $5 every time I went to the store. All I could say is that was better than minimum wage was. At the time, it was $3.35 per hour, and I was making close to double in fifteen minutes.

Mook was his name, and boy, did he have some nice teeth. Also a nice smile to go along with it. We developed a friendship just from my daily store runs until one day he asked how old I was. I told him I was twelve years old. I just had a birthday a week earlier. So he asked if I had a boyfriend. I said, "No, my mother said wait until I was sixteen years old before I could date." Then he asked, "Have you ever had sex before?" I asked why. He then said, "Because I want to know if you are a virgin." I said yes, but this was a great big ole *lie.* Hell, he had no way of finding out.

Before I knew it, he was all over me, kissing, licking, and sucking me from my head to my toes. Within a split second, he was inside of me, pumping in and out of me like some kind of animal. I believe he had a good time. I can't say much for myself because before I could even get into it, everything was all over. Homeboy was breathing hard with a big-ass smile on his face. I was like, *shit* not again.

This sex shit really is not all I thought it was cracked up to be from the movies and books I have read in the past about it. You see during my visits to my great aunt and uncle home here in Detroit. I would go into their upstairs bedrooms where their older sons slept and snoop around I found that they had all sorts of X- rated books like Penthouse & Hustler magazines and movies called Big Black Pussy or Horney Black Girls up there so I would look through them and watch adult movies while everyone else would be outside playing.

I pulled my pants up and opened the van door, said 'bye, and closed the door. I went to the attic to get myself some fresh panties so I could take a bath. Once inside the bathroom, I made up my mind that I didn't want to do it again because it was not fun for me at all.

I lay back in the tub and felt worthless. Like a piece of meat for the second time. *No more sex for me!* Leon did me the exact same way when I was eleven, just a few months after I started my period. I let him talk me into giving him some, and he just fucked me and got with another girl that he really liked.

Can you believe this? I'm less than thirteen years old, and I have already had sex with two guys? Why was I so promiscuous?

Something had to have happened to me as a young child to make me want to be touched in such sexual ways. I think about this often, but I can't figure out who it could have been.

Game time! Only twelve years old but old enough to know that this is not what the men really want from a woman. What they want is for a woman to hold on to it and make them earn the privilege of getting up inside of you. Now I fully understand how it all goes and these niggas are going to have to pay from now on. Even just for looking at Ms. Lesia Lipz. Someone has just created a fucking monster. The cat and dog game is about to begin.

It's now February of 1979. I haven't spoken to Mook since the police took the entire van full to the jail for selling drugs. I've just been going to school and coming straight back to the house up to the attic to do my homework and have a few words of conversation with my aunt Peaches. My routine had changed since we first moved here. I felt a lot more comfortable especially since my aunt and I were now talking from time to time.

I got to know a little bit about her, and I would imagine she got to know a little bit more about me as well.

I learned that she was just as unhappy as I was with our environment and the family as a whole. We both had some anger issues toward Granny even though she was her daughter. She felt mistreated just like I felt. So now we have something in common to converse over. Peaches was five years older than me, and she was my mother's youngest sister. I began looking at her more like an older sister than an aunt. I assume it was due to our closeness in age. I really like her as a person now. She is not as bad as I thought she was at all.

Since having sex with Mook, I hadn't noticed that I had not had a period since December. I guess I was so caught up in wondering whatever happened to him and trying to get my mind off him. Plus, remembering how Leon had done almost the same thing to me along with trying to build up my strength as a young woman making sure this shit never happened to me ever again. I simply forgot all about my menstrual cycle since I hated coming on anyway. I was a heavy bleeder and suffered serious cramps every month. Deep down inside, I may have been happy not to see it.

While getting dressed for school one morning, I began having sharp stomach pains in the lower part of my stomach. I thought to myself, *Oh damn, it's about to start.* I put three sanitary napkins in my purse and went on to school. While riding the public bus, more pain hit me, but I continued on with my day. Just before it was time to go home, I felt it coming down. Boy, was I happy. *At least*, I think to myself, *now I know I'm not pregnant.* I took the bus home, and I thanked God that it was Friday, so I have the weekend to deal with this bleeding shit plus we will be out of school for winter break. I get in the house, go straight to the bathroom, and there is blood all over the place. My panties and my pants are full of blood.

I wash up, put on a new pad and my pajamas. I put all my soiled clothes in the washer and got in the bed for the remainder of the night. I was back and forth to the bathroom. I changed my pad at least three times throughout the night.

Something was very different about my period. This time there were small blood clots dropping into the toilet, and I was having pains so much stronger than normal. I remained silent about it for a few days before I found the nerves to tell my aunt Peaches. She said, "My period changes up from time to time also, so don't panic unless you see something like a big blood clot or the bleeding begins to run like water." I said okay and kept a close watch for those two things.

After about ten days, I was still bleeding, but no one seemed to notice. I even asked Mama for money to buy another bag of pads. She just gave me the money and asked no questions. I continued to bleed. The flow never changed, but I was beginning to feel really weak. Boom! Like something exploding deep inside my womb is what it felt like.

When all of a sudden I tried to get out of the bed but my legs were extremely weak, I fell to the floor and crawled to the bathroom across the hall from the room where I had been sleeping for the past few days so I could be closer to the bathroom.

My body began to sweat from head to toe. I pulled myself across the hallway floor with all the strength I had left inside me. It's about 4:30 a.m. Everyone in the house was fast asleep. I tried to be as quiet as I possibly could. I didn't want to wake anyone up. So I held back the tears until I made it onto the bathroom floor. I reached up as I sat behind the door to lock it. The last thing I wanted was for someone to walk in and see me like this. I pulled myself up onto the toilet, and once I got my pajama pants and my panties down, a pain so unbearable hit me. I bit down on my bottom lip as something so excruciating fell down, through and out of my young and so unprepared body. There was a large splash into the toilet; blood poured everywhere.

This was a pain I have never had my whole life. I knew right away something was seriously wrong. I rolled tissue around my hand, large as a boxing glove, and placed it in my panties to hold all the blood that was pouring out of my body.

I slide to the floor in front of the toilet onto my knees and turned around slowly to view the big odd-shaped blood-filled piece of tissue in the toilet, I reached inside to pick it up. It felt like flesh, very soft but mushy. I couldn't figure out anything that it looked like, but I felt a lot better that it was out of me. I studied it for a few minutes more, then I flushed it down the toilet. There was a knock at the door shortly after. It was my aunt Peaches. She had to use it bad. I was like "Hold on, here I come," but she was like "Hurry up, I'm about to pee on myself." So I opened the door, and she saw all the blood on the floor and toilet.

She was in a panic and called my mama's name, "San! San! Get up and come to the bathroom. Something is wrong with Lesia. It's blood all over the place," and the entire house was awake in two minutes. Granny called the ambulance. They took me to the hospital. I was there for a few days. We found out that I had a miscarriage. Also I was about two to three months pregnant.

Once back home, everyone looked at me with great disgust. They wanted to know who in the world has taken advantage of a twelve-year-old girl. In the house, I was questioned by everybody. "Who did this to you?" "Was it this person or that person?" I never gave a name or said a word about it. It wasn't long before I was put on lockdown. I had to be watched at all times. I couldn't even go to the store by myself. No one trusted me anymore. Mama looked at me different also. She began not coming home after work. She didn't even call to let us know she was okay or even where she was. Granny was getting sick of us being there.

One morning, Mama didn't come home, so I knocked on my granny's bedroom door and asked if she had heard from her. She yelled through the door, "Little girl, I have not heard from your mammie! She may be somewhere laid up with some nigga. She's all right. Take your ass to school. And don't knock back on my door!" I took a deep breath and walked away, knowing I wanted to kick it down and slap the shit out of her.

What grandmother says something like that to a child about their mother? She was just a *mean* person.

I got ready for school and left in a hurry. Tears poured down my face as my sister Tonia and I walked to the bus stop. Tonia asked why I let her get to me all the time. I told her she would never understand since she treated her like a princess. Much to my surprise, Tonia said, "I do notice how she treats you." I was shocked. She then said, "But what can I do about it, Lesia?" I looked at her and said, "Nothing, I guess." We got on the bus and went to school. Tonia stopped me before entering the school and said, "Don't worry, we will be moving soon. Mama told me. So it won't be much longer." I was pleased to hear that. We walked inside and went our separate ways.

I couldn't wait for school to be over that day. I met up with Tonia to catch the bus home, hoping Mama was there, but she had not made it from work yet. I waited up until night, still no Mama.

I was on the phone with my daddy when the second line rang. I answered. It was Mama. She said, "Tell Tonia and Tony to put their clothes in a bag. I'm on my way to pick you all up. We're moving out of there tonight."

I clicked back to my daddy and told him I would call him back later so I could do what she told me to do. I didn't say a word to Peaches or Granny about it.

Mama pulled up shortly after the call with her friend and called us as she always did according to our ages, "Tonia, Lesia, and Tony, come downstairs. Do you have your things ready?"

"Yes," we said in sequence.

"Okay, go to the car. I need to talk to your granny. I will be right out." Minutes later, they were outside, yelling and screaming at each other. "You're a poor excuse for a mother," said my mama, then Granny said, "At least my children know where I am at all times." My mother then said, "Well, I had no idea where you were for sixteen years, lady," and walked off the porch.

Granny stood there for a brief spell in silence then said, "I left you with my mother who I knew would take care of you well." My mom retaliated with these final words, "Yes, she did. I wish I could say the same about you with mine!"

We drove off. I looked out the rear window of the car to see Granny staring at the car as it went down the street. Once we hit the corner to turn, she went back inside of the house. We sat quietly, listening to my mother talk to her friend about Granny leaving her as a child to be with her husband who was also the father of all her siblings. She also told her she felt my granny hated she ever had her.

Her friend's name was Joann. They worked together at BC/BS for many years. We pulled up in front of Joann's house which looked very nice from the outside. I had no idea this was the new temporary location, but it had to be better than Granny's house. Right?

The Journey Unfolds

We moved in with my mother's girlfriend. Needless to say, it made me miss living with Granny. At least her house was clean. This woman lived in a two-family unit upstairs, full of cockroaches, rats, and the newborn mice. I could not sleep with worry of having a roach stuck in my ear or being bitten by one of the rats. Somebody please tell me, am I asleep? Or has my mother lost her *damn* mind? When you're from the hood, you learn real quickly to make the best of your circumstances, so I and Tonia tried to clean up the house in hopes of this making a difference, but it didn't. Lucky for us, this stay did not last for long but long enough that we met the neighborhood teenagers. We did not get along with the girls on the block, but the guys were like zombies. They were bumping into each other trying to get our names or number.

Out of them all, we connected with our homeboy for life Fella. He was a good-looking guy with a medium build, eighteen years old, but he had one leg. This guy could do anything a guy with two legs could do, but better. We never got the real story on what happened to his leg, but it really didn't matter. He took us on as his little sisters and brother. Fella had a thing for Tonia like all guys did, but she used it to her advantage. He brought her whatever she wanted, and he looked out for my brother and me also. (We lived here for only four months.)

My mother was beaten by a local taxicab driver after work one night on payday. Everyone in Detroit knew that BC/BS got paid on the second and fourth Thursday of the month. After taking her to cash her check, he beat her and threw her out of the cab near the hospital. She suffered from multiple blows to the head. She had over one hundred stitches. After a short stay in the hospital, she was released, and we moved into my daddy's apartment. Daddy had a very clean place, and he cooked every day, something we all loved. It was all good as long as neither of them were drinking.

We knew this stay was not going to last for long before Daddy would start drinking. Whenever he got drunk, he would try to force Mama to have sex with him. She got tired of fighting him off. She was not interested in Daddy anymore. They had not slept together for years. Daddy was so pissed off that he put us out of his place. Now that's a nigga for you. (We lived here for two months.)

My grandfather Angus lived on the second floor in the same building as Daddy. He told my mother to bring us up to his place until she found us a place of our own. He said he would give her the first months' rent if she could come up with the deposit. Now it is the spring of 1980. Mama found a two-bedroom apartment in the middle of Saigon (just a figure of speech). It was the worst neighborhood she could have ever chosen to live in—on Monterey between Dexter and Linwood, an area in Detroit known for drugs and murders. These niggas were selling crack cocaine in the middle of the street right in front of our house like an assembly line. (We lived in my daddy's building for three months, and I lived with Mama for four years.)

The only perk to this location was I bumped into Mook at the corner store, and he told me that he lived right around the corner.

This put a whole new outlook on things as far as I was concerned. We learned a lot about the streets in this area and did most of our growing up here. Mook and I started spending time together, but something was different about him. He was much more hyper than he used to be. Rumors had it that he was on drugs, and you know I did not want to believe that, but it turned out to be true. Mook was hooked on powder cocaine—one of the same drugs he had been selling since he was twelve years old. Well, there was no way in hell that I was going to be dating a drug addict, so I had to leave him alone. We remained good friends. We would still hug whenever we came in contact. I just prayed that he would overcome his addiction some day.

My days consisted of going to school, coming straight home, and praying that I didn't get shot or raped on my journey.

The summer was slowly approaching. I was sitting on the front porch, reading a book, when this older guy from directly across the street came out on his top porch. He raised one of his legs to rest his foot on the banister and one arm held on to the awning and just smiled at me. Of course I acted like I didn't see him. The ice cream truck was coming down the street. Tonia and I went to get some ice cream and guess who shows up. The guy from across the street. And once again, who is he looking at? My sister. I have to admit, I did not blame him. They spoke to each other then he said, "Do you have a boyfriend?" She said with an attitude, "What's it to you?" His whole facial expression changed, then he said, "Well, excuse me." She said, "You're excused," got her ice cream, and walked away. That let me know she was not interested in him. I smiled. Then he said, "What are you smiling at?" I said, "Nothing." He said, "You must be smiling at something." So I said, "It was an inside joke." He said, "Well, do you want to share it with me?" Then I said, "I'd rather not." I got my ice cream and walked away.

I was smiling because I loved the way my sister handled boys. She was the mean one. She didn't take any shit, and I was the nice easygoing one who liked everybody. I just wanted everyone to love each other and all get along. But Tonia, she did not care one way or the other. A few days later, he decided to step across the street. He rang the doorbell. I answered. He said, "Hey, my name is Jeff." I said, "My name is Lesia." He asked, "Can you come outside on the porch?" We both went outside together, and we just talked for hours about the neighborhood along with other things. It was a really nice conversation. Before long, Jeff and I had become an item. We were inseparable. He was a few years older, but that was okay. Jeff was the youngest of ten children, and his parents were older, so he acted a lot older than he was. But I guess that was to be expected. His older siblings were in their thirties. I fell in love with him and his family because they were the family that everyone wanted. They were a very close-knit family. They all stopped by Mama Perry's house for dinner every day, and they had family day on the weekend to play Po-Ke-No or BidWiz.

I loved being over there, and they all loved me. I was treated just like family right from the start. Mama Perry allowed me to spend time in Jeff's bedroom without any problems. After all, he was almost an adult, but I was only thirteen years old. Since the miscarriage, I was no longer sexually active.

My mama had threatened me that if I ever got pregnant again, I would be raising the child by myself because she was not raising any babies, so I better keep my legs closed. After going through something so traumatic, trust me, having sex or having a baby was the furthest thing on my mind. Jeff was so understanding and patient with me. He never forced sex on me. He respected me so much. I knew he was getting sex outside of our relationship but said nothing about it. We had such a strong grounded relationship that the sexual part never really came up. We loved each other just for who we were, not for sex.

We both agreed that we would wait until my sixteenth birthday to have our first encounter with sex, and we did just that. Three years had passed, and my birthday was drawing near when I asked Mama if she could take me to get birth control like I promised her I would do. She said, "Okay, we still have a few months to take care of that." I replied, "Well, I know, but it takes a while to get into your system." She then said, "If you were able to wait this long, you can wait until you turn eighteen." I said, "I'm not waiting until I am eighteen. My boyfriend has been patient. I have allowed him to sleep with other women all this time, and I refuse to make him wait any longer!" I stormed out the door and went around the corner to a friend's house to call him at work and tell him what had just happened. He was calm and told me that it was all right to go back home. We will talk about it when he got off work.

I waited for him, and once he got home, he came over. I could not believe that I was madder than he was. He then said, "It's no big deal, Lesia. I love you, so if we have to wait, we will just wait."

I thought to myself, *This is some bullshit. I be damned if I am waiting two more years before giving my man some of this pussy. How long do you think I was going to be okay with him fucking other bitches?* It has been as long as it was going to be for me. Tension was all throughout our house. I stopped talking to Mama for a few weeks only unless I had to, but now it was only a few weeks before my birthday, so I began talking back to her gradually because I had a plan to give up some pussy to Jeff on my birthday anyway. His sister would be out of town, so we were going to be house sitting for the weekend during the day together, and he would bring me home before 11:00 p.m.

Jeff asked if it was okay for me to go check on her house with him. Mama agreed. She said, "Just have her back before 11:00 p.m." We got to his sister's house. We opened some Golden Champale, smoked some weed, and it happened. It was like I never had sex before. It was totally different with Jeff. It was full of passion. My whole body shook all over, and we both cried together. From Joy & Excitement. It was a beautiful experience. Jeff pulled out. I saw his come and everything. Your girl had just made love for the first time. He said he would not get me pregnant. I trusted him too.

Wow! I missed my period and started freaking out. I was one week late for my period, so I let Jeff know. He began to panic and decided that we had to tell my mama. It was Christmas Eve when we told her. Believing she may not take it so hard since it was Christmas time. Shit. She told him to leave and beat the hell out of me. We were out of school for Christmas vacation, which made the punishment even worse. Mama had me washing clothes, dishes, mopping floors, and washing walls. Jeff tapped on my bedroom window to tell me he would be giving me the money for my senior dues, class ring, and senior pictures. That following Monday, we were returning to school.

Monday came. It was 6:00 a.m. I walked as light as I could down the long hallway. I had to pass Mama's bedroom door. I made it to the dining room.

I cracked the front door and waited on Jeff to come across the street with the money. He came, gave me the money, kissed me, and left for work.

I closed the door, turned around, and there was Mama. She looked like the devil was in her eyes. She put her hand out, and I said, "What?" She said, "Did Jeff just give you some money?" I said, "Yes, for my senior dues and things." She said, "Well, you can just give it here because the gas is about to be shut off." I looked at her like, "Do you think I really give a fuck?" Jeff had been taking care of me for three years. Mama had not done anything for me since I got with him. So honestly, I didn't give a fuck, and I told her it was not my problem. She grabbed my wrist and snatched the money from my hand and said, "I don't give a fuck about all that shit you saying you need to do either."

We started fighting like two broads on the streets.

It wasn't long before Tonia woke up and tried to break us up. Before I knew it, both of them were hitting me. Mama's man at the time pulled everyone apart or, should I say, pulled them off me. Mama told me to wash dishes before I left for school. I went in the kitchen and began slamming dishes and making all types of noises with them. I heard her coming back down the hallway really fast. She grabbed my head and snatched a whole handful of my hair, then she put her arm around my neck got a fork and placed it to my jugular vein. She said, "Bitch, you gone make me kill your ass. I screamed let go of my hair. It's simply one too many bitches up in this motherfucking house."

Mama said, "You're right. That would be you, and it's time for you to go." My mama and sister whooped my ass. They pulled patches of my hair out, scratched my face all up, busted my lip, and kicked me out of the house with my pajama's still on, and threw my purse and coat out the door to me. I left hollering and screaming all the way down the block at them, telling them that they would be sorry they would never see me again, and I was going to get both of them back for what they had done to me. Blood was dripping from my face. I had bald spots all over my head. I looked like I was just robbed and beaten by a gang. Once I got to my girlfriend's house, I called Jeff, and he came to get me. We then called his sister, Melvine, and told her what had happen between my mother and me. She told Jeff we both could come live with her until I graduated in June.

Living with his sister was the best thing that ever could have happened to me. She was so cool and very understanding to young adults. She taught me many important things that has helped me along the way, such as always have your own, never depend on a man, life is what you make it, you have to work hard for whatever you want, it makes you appreciate it more, and last but not least, it is better that two people work together than it is for one person working by oneself. All these things are key factors in my daily living today. She helped me get a job where she worked, which happened to be the same insurance company my mother worked for. It was a co-op position, and my very first job making my own money. This was awesome. I got paid biweekly. She helped me open a bank account to place all my money into so I could get a vehicle of my own.

I was asked if I wanted to be full time, but I had to present a diploma or GED before the end of March. This left me with a big decision to make. I still had two months before I graduated, and I had to complete all my classes to get my diploma. So I talked it over with Jeff, and we decided I should go ahead and take my GED test in this one-day program because this was a good-paying job that could become a lifetime career for me and I should not pass this up. I took the test and passed, got the position, and began working full time. I worked a lot of overtime as well; my checks were grown-ass woman checks. I saved to get my car, and Jeff and I got our own place too. We moved into an upscale high-rise apartment near the university. 5500 Trumbull #305 our first apartment that we called our own. We didn't have regular metal keys we used key cards to enter our building it was something new at the time. It made me feel important like I had accomplished something at the ripe age of 17. We had 24 hour surveillance along with an armed officer at our front desk. I purchased my very first vehicle a 1980 powder blue Chevy Chevette. I loved it because it belonged to me.

Becoming a Woman

Jeff and I were a couple for seven years before we had our first baby boy. We named him Jeffrey Jr. We nicknamed him JP. He weighed 6'11. There were problems with the pregnancy. We were expecting twins until our sixth month when Dr. Choi told us that the ultrasound only showed one baby. We were all stunned. Also I had developed a very serious infection that needed to be treated prior to delivering the baby.

We later discovered that we indeed were having twins; the one that did not survive was stillborn and was also back to back with JP. I delivered in an upside down position similar to doing the bicycle due to my womb is tilted. The doctors told me that the opening to deliver my baby was closer to my buttocks. I vomited and experienced the worse labor pains ever for over fourteen hours before my son was born. I delivered naturally nothing of pain.

After the delivery, my doctor explained to us the reason why one of the babies did not survive. It was called the invisible baby. This happens with twins. One of them takes all the nutrients from the other. This stops the babies' development, so she was something like dissolved tissue inside of me, and this is what caused the infection. We were also asked if we wanted to see the baby but we refused. Jeff felt that I did not need any bad memories of our first child's birth. I agreed, but we were told that it was a girl.

It wasn't long before our relationship began to change. It was more so that I was changing, not Jeff. I wanted to find out what things did I really like to do and what my personal interests were. I had been with this man since I was a kid, and everything we had done for the past seven years were all the things that Jeff enjoyed doing. I just followed along, but now I needed to know what my own likes and dislikes are. It was time for me to make some decision of my own.

Once JP turned four months, I told Jeff I no longer wanted to be in a relationship with him anymore. He didn't argue it at all. I believe he may have wanted some freedom himself.

We said it would just be temporary, and he promised to always be there for me. I moved in with my best friend only six blocks over from Jeff's house. I felt safe not being far away from him. He had been my protector for a very long time.

Wow, I can't believe it. I was a single woman for the first time in life. It's now 1987. I had not long turned twenty years old. I am a woman now. I got a job as an assistant manager at Payless Shoe Source and a second part-time job at Kentucky Fried Chicken to pay my bills. Jeff still had my back for any needs I could not handle. Jeff was a great father. I could not have found a better man to have my first child with. We tried to work things out between us, but the flame had blown out between us. We decided to raise our son and remain the best of friends. That's exactly what we did.

I spent most of my time working during the day, and JP was being watched by my best friend Courtnay. She was his godmother, plus she had no children of her own at the time, so she was able to give all her attention to him. Soon Court started working also, then I began paying our other girlfriend who also lived with us for babysitting. Our place was nice and big. There was a living room, dining room, kitchen, one bathroom, with three bedrooms and a basement. My favorite feature of the house was the screened-in front porch. We could sleep out there on hot nights.

I had my telephone installed in my bedroom that was in the far back end of the house. I wanted to be in the back to have a little more privacy. I continued on with my daily routine, to work, back home, time with my son, to bed, and start all over again. It was nice to wake on the weekends and be able to sit on the front porch early in the morning with a hot cup of coffee or tea. To just hear the birds singing and smelling the freshness of the early morning air. Being single was something I wished I had done before I had a baby but it's too late to have those thoughts.

My son, JP, was my joy. I was so proud to be a mother. He wasn't a crybaby; thank God for that. I changed his clothes at least three times a day. He had to be clean at all times. Where I went, he went if it wasn't to work.

We would stop by Jeff's house when we were out for a visit, which became shorter and shorter by the time summer hit. It was my first summer without having to be sitting out in the sun at one field or another. Jeff played every sport there was it seemed. He was very athletic and in good shape. All my friends told me all the time, "Girl, Jeff know he be looking good. All muscular built and fit." I knew it too. I just would smile and think to myself, *Yeah, he is, isn't he?*

One visit to Jeff's, things were different. He kept us in the living room, which was unusual. Later, I found out he was dating someone. And he did not know how to tell me. Once we met, I felt she was more of his type. She wasn't from the street life as I was. She was very nice plus my son seemed to like her. That's what was the most important factor.

Now I felt better about moving on with life completely and began dating shortly afterward. I dated here and there but found no one that I saw a future with at the time, so I remained single for the entire summer. This was a good choice I made, not having to answer to a man, coming and going as I pleased. *Freedom!* This is what I feel, and I like it. Being the best mother in the world was my goal, taking care of him and myself before anything or anybody. "Do not have any other man around my son unless it becomes serious but wait as long as possible. Now stick to it, Lesia," is what I thought to myself.

Huh, yes, the devil is always busy.

New Experiences

Just before Easter, my sister called to ask if she and her kids could come stay for a weekend. I told her that I would have to talk it over with my roommates. After all, I just moved there myself. They were both okay with the idea, not knowing that once Tonia was there, she had no plans on leaving. Monday morning came. I said, "Tonia girl, when do you want me to take yawl home?" She starts crying and asking why she can't stay there with me. I told her this was not my house. She said, "What if I ask them if I can stay for a while?" I said, "You can ask" (just knowing they would say there was not any room for them). Both of them said they did not mind if they stayed until she found a place of her own. It was really because they were afraid of her. All my friends were afraid of Tonia.

Now the house is packed, eight people living in a three-bedroom flat. Tonia was not looking for a place at all. She started dating this guy, who appeared to be very nice. He worked at the automobile assembly plant, and made really good money. Before long our house became the party house. First Tonia, then Tony began falling through whenever he wanted, then my little cousin Trecia needed somewhere to stay. Every night between eight to ten people sleeping there. Our place was now becoming the Du Drop Inn. Even though it was crowded, we started off having a great time together.

My brother, Tony, was the weed man. All the adults smoked marijuana except Courtnay. Since he was stopping by often, we smoked for free. We never knew Tony was an in-the-closet 51 smoker, which means he would lace weed with crack cocaine and roll them up together in cigarette paper before smoking it but no one knew it. Shortly afterward, Tony would stop by with the joints already rolled up and begin selling them to us for $5 a joint. We had no idea we were smoking another form of cocaine. We all thought he just had some really good weed. Before long we were all addicted to 51s just like Tony.

Within weeks, Tony admitted the truth to all of us about what we were really smoking. He just laughed about it, as if it were a joke. We were already high when he told us. Everyone just sat in silence for a while. Then I asked, "What did you say, Tony?" He answered, "You know, yawl have been smoking 51s for the last couple of weeks." He continued laughing, but by this time, it didn't matter. We liked it and just continued smoking. (This is why there are so many people hooked on drugs today. Most of them have been introduced by someone they trust.) We were getting high from sun up to sun down. It was so bad that we started keeping the blinds closed all day long.

Crackheads prefer being in the dark, and we were becoming paranoid. It was not long before the guy that supplied my brother with the drugs became suspicious because Tony's money started coming up short.

He approached me with the question, "Is Tony getting high?" I told him that I didn't know. I told my brother that he was becoming suspicious of him getting high. Tony left one day and said he would be back, but he never returned, but he did call to say he was all right. He moved to Pontiac where he thought he would be safe and clean up his act with the drugs. But Pontiac had changed from how it used to be; drugs had taken over the small city. Moving to Pontiac was no longer a safe haven if anything it made his habit worse.

TONIA

Tonia did not like many people, but those that she did like, she loved. A couple of the guys on the block liked Tonia, but she was not interested in any of them. This pissed them off. The morning after a few unfriendly words were exchanged between my sister and them, her boyfriend's car was vandalized. They broke out his windows, flatted his tires, and even stole his radio. We found out who did it by one of the people living in our house. She slept on the front screened-in porch that night, and the noise woke her up, so she peeked over the banister to witness the guys across the street damaging his car.

We believed him to be a nice and quiet guy, but he flipped out over his car. He made a police report then made a phone call to have his car picked up threw his insurance company, then called his boys to tell them what had taken place with his car. That evening, he and his friends damn near burned the entire block down. They drove up the block shooting and tossing firebombs in houses. A total of four houses caught fire that night.

Out of the four houses, one belonged to the grandparents of the guys on the block. Their grandfather passed away from smoke inhalation. This was so serious now someone has been murdered! My next-door neighbor whispered, trying to warn me to get my son out of the house before it got dark the next day, and I did. Investigators walked up and down the block, knocking on doors, trying to get any information on why all this had taken place. I left all my stuff and got the hell out of there.

I told both of my girlfriends to leave too. One of them was so strung out on the 51s that her stupid ass stayed in the house with her son. She said she had nowhere to go. Later that night, our house was set on fire, with my girlfriend and her son inside. They made it out of the house through the back door. We lost all our belongings.

The police escorted us inside to see if we could salvage anything the following day, but I slept in the back room and this is where the fire was started, so it was in the worst condition. Now we all had to start over. I moved back in with Jeff for a few months, then I found an apartment on his street. Courtnay and I moved back together, but our other girlfriend ended up being found murdered later that year. She had become a crack whore. Her body was found in the trash can behind one of the neighborhood liquor stores. Her murder was never solved. It seemed that no one really cared about a person hooked on crack being murdered during those times, especially the police.

After finding out about my girlfriend, I knew it was time to stop smoking 51s and get my shit together. It had only been for a season but it seemed a whole lot longer than that. In the end I had been smoking that shit for long enough that I lost a friend along with all my belongings. Back to my old habit of working, coming home to my son, relaxing, and getting ready for another day of the same routine again.

Tonia and her kids were all over the city following behind the guy she was dating. Until he finally decided to get them a place of their own. They moved into a four family apartment not far from Dexter. Tonia had called to give me the address but I didn't hear from her for weeks since she moved in so I decided to stop by for a visit I had Jeff drop JP and I off one sunny day. I tried calling before I went but again no answer. Once we arrived Jeff helped us into the house JP was in his carrier seat. We were both dressed in all white this day. Tonia opened the door with a surprising look but allowed me inside. I told Jeff I would call him when we were ready to be picked up but I planned on staying for a few hours.

Jeff left and Tonia and I gave each other a big hug then I asked why hadn't she called me or answered my calls. She replied because he takes the phone with him in the morning when he leaves for work because he doesn't want me dealing with anyone in our family. My mouth dropped I said, "What kind of shit is that?" Tonia didn't look good at all to me. This was first in our lifetime. I asked her "What's up Tonia?" She said, I have to get out of here before he kills me. Then she starts telling me how he hates me for no reason at all. He says that you think you are all that (meaning better than other people) but I told him that you were not like that at all. So you have to leave before he comes home from work. It now 3pm what time does he get off? At 3pm she said. I was tripping out over all that she just told me. So I picked up my cell phone to call Jeff but it was no answer he was playing baseball. I left a message on his voicemail of all she told me. Then waited for his return call. Before long this fool of hers pulls up to the house with his music blasting so loud. Tonia began to panic she said, Go sit on the porch until Jeff comes I said are you crazy it's hot as hell outside. I'm sitting here until he comes.

He walks into the house looks right at me and says, "What are you doing over here? I said, to visit my sister. He then said, "You are not welcome here." I said, "well I'm about to leave as soon as my ride gets here". Go outside and wait he said. I said, "Not with my baby in that heat". He began pushing me out the door I tried fighting him back before he punched me right between the eyes in the nose. I heard my nose break I was passed out cold. Not sure of how long I was out but I was awaken to my sister hanging over the top balcony porch of their apartment and the kids were on the opposite side of the top porch on the neighbor's porch. Blood was all over me and my son, my baby was crying from all the confusion. I ran down the hall to her bathroom to clean the blood off of my face so I could see clearly. Once back into the front end of the apartment I noticed everyone was gone my sister was down the street close to the corner being beat by her man. I reached for my phone to call Brock he answered I explained what was going on and where I was he was there in a flash to my rescue. He came in with his friend they helped me get all my belonging and Tonia's kids from the neighbor's. Put us in the car and we could not find Tonia anywhere.

We took the kids to my mothers and I went to the hospital indeed my nose was broken. Later that evening they back tracked to Tonia's and they were both there. I know they whooped his ass good and Tonia was bought back to mama's house.

She later revealed to me that he starting fighting her once they moved in the apartment he was a jealous and insecure man just like my daddy was. Tonia said he would always tell her you not as pretty as you think you are baby. He was going to beat her to ugly if he could.

Tonia and her children moved in the unit upstairs from us. Tonia was hooked on the drugs too but not bad enough to sell her body. She started doing disappearing acts and leaving the kids at the house, which caused me to lose my job. I was calling off at the last minute to avoid the kids being left alone. My son was now a year old, and I wanted to spend as much time as possible with him, my nephew Jamell and niece Tesia at the time it appeared I was all they had.

Tonia was a product of a good girl gone bad. When we were in grade school, she was one of the smartest girls in the class. She participated in all kinds of activities up until my granny changed her life forever by telling her that Larry was her father. She turned into an untrusting, insecure person from that point on. She felt she could not trust anyone except me. She also felt that she could not show any affection for anyone except for me. This all was to protect her heart. Once our granny told the truth, she just felt like she couldn't trust my mama or granny anymore. I became her only friend.

My granny embedded in her head over the years that men would take care of her. This also destroyed my sister. She never wanted to work.

She just lived one day at a time without any worry or concern. This did have one advantage for her. It kept her looking young.

I was the worrier, and I also looked the oldest. I grew up feeling sorry for my sister. I could feel her pain, but I didn't like the fact that she let this one mishap in her life take over her life to this degree.

Even after having her children, she showed little to no motivation. My mother, along with the children's grandmother, were the providers for her household. I finally talked her into taking on a job with me in Pontiac at a nursing home. I taught her all about vitals and patient care, and she did a fairly good job for a while, but it only lasted a few months before she quit. Living a productive life was not in Tonia's plan. We talked about everything. We were closer than the average sisters. As a child, I wanted nothing more than to look like and be like my big sister.

Things got so bad with her disappearing acts that my Aunt Peaches, came to take the kids so I could go back to work. Tonia showed up after a really long stay away, and we had our first fistfight since we were about nine and ten years old. I just could not take it anymore, seeing my sister looking so small and smelling so file. After that fight, Tonia snapped out of it. She got her kids back and left the shit alone. She met a new guy and had her third baby. It was a girl. She named her Tamisha. Shortly after her birth, they moved in together. For the first time in years, Tonia appeared happy.

My Brother Tony: The First Male that I Spoiled

Tony Bone is what we called him as a child. He was my only brother and happened to be the youngest of my siblings by my mama. He is two years behind me in age. My sister and I began spoiling him right from the time he came home for the hospital and we found out he was a boy. Plus Mama wasn't going to have it any other way. Tony was sort of on the short side. All while he was growing up, his hair was a very light sandy-brown color just like Mama's. He was a fighter from the age of six. His teachers used to hate to see him coming. A true boy, he was rough and tough and had no age limit on whom he would fight.

Not a summer went by that he wasn't either in the hospital or had some type of body injury. One winter, he decided after watching Evel Knievel on television. That he could do anything that he saw Evel Knievel do. He got a ladder out the garage and had his friends help him take his bike on top of the garage. Then they found a long wood board and placed it from our garage to the neighbor's garage. Then he placed his bike on the board and tried to ride it from one garage to the next, but the wood collapsed in the middle, and he fell to the concrete and busted his head wide open. Blood was everywhere. He was unconscious. His head was swollen to the size of a small watermelon when we got to the hospital.

He was out of commission for a couple of day and was right back at it before long you would think that after an incident like that he would have had enough of the injuries but Oh No, not Tony Bone. He needed another injury before summer I assumed. It was spring time shortly before Easter Tony and his friends who were always much older than he was were playing a game called "chicken" when they have to bump into each another's tires of their bikes trying to knock them off.

But Tony was hit so hard that he shot straight through a fence and his mouth got caught onto the wire and torn his bottom lip really bad. He needed several stitches to repair the tear. He was unable to talk for a good while.

Tonia and I were responsible for taking care of him while Mama worked. We had to blend up his food because his teeth also went through his lip, so they were sewn together to the midsection. They left his right side open so he could suck on a straw to take in his pureed food. We did this for the entire spring. We bathed him, dressed him, and fed him until he got better.

Being surrounded by women who catered to him constantly turned my little brother into the kind of guy that felt every woman in his path had to treat him the same as we did.

Tony had a girlfriend by the age of twelve too, they were serious about each other and also having sex. We found out his girlfriend was pregnant when he was only thirteen and she was only fourteen years old. The parents made her get an abortion, for what reason, I'm not sure because she was right back pregnant within a year. She had this one, my brother's first child, a boy, when he was only still a boy himself. There wasn't much they could do for the baby at the time. Her mother pretty much raised him for the beginning years of his life.

When Tony turned fifteen years old, he started selling other harder drugs to help out on supporting his son. He had been living with them since the baby was born. I had not seen my brother but only a few times for the past four years since I moved away from home. When we finally caught up with each other, they had a second son, and I had my first son. My siblings and I agreed that we would start spending more time together like we used to do. From that day forth, the three of us kept in touch almost every day.

My brother had a best friend named Punkin who was murdered when they were sixteen years old.

We found out later that my brother was expected to be there with him at the time it happened. Tony was very different after this happened, more angry and untrustworthy. His determination to get out of the neighborhood grew stronger. He would not have his children grow up in the hood like we did. One thing for sure was if he called you friend, he was one until the end. Whoever had him as a friend was very lucky?

He made a promise that he would purchase his first property before he was twenty-five years old for his children. And he did just that. This would be a big accomplishment for him, but he was still not ready to be in a committed relationship. Tony was a womanizer. He loved the attention that he received whenever he walked in a room. All the girls loved Tony because he was funny, handsome, and overly confident—all the things women wanted in a man. This is also why he fathered four children in one year by four different women. He was a good man as far as paying the bills, but as far as being home or taking time out with the kids, it was another whole story.

Paying the bills but not putting in the time was something he saw our daddy do, which is not enough to a kid. He learned to be a man from the street, which was not a good thing, but he did the best he could as a young man. Being a guy with some money was all the women wanted back in the eighties. As long as a guy had some game and a car, he was able to get any girl he wanted. All everybody wanted was a way out, and so did Tony. He hustled in a few small cities throughout Michigan. He got caught up in a situation in one of these cities at a motel. It was all over the news—a big drug bust.

He got arrested and needed to be bailed out on a $50,000 personal bond at 10 percent. He had to stay in jail for close to a week before Mook went to pay the money so he could get out. This was a big scare for him. He knew jail was somewhere he didn't want to be.

After that episode, he was very careful about what he did and who he did it with. Most of the guys in our neighborhood believed that going to jail made them look tuff. But my brother didn't need to go to jail be known as being tuff.

I worried about my little brother even more than ever now because the drug game was changing by the second. People were becoming scandalous just to get high off a piece of crack cocaine. I made it my business to call him several times throughout the day to check on him for myself and for our mama. One night, I received a call from Tony. He was whispering, saying some guys had him at a house in Pontiac working off a debt from a bad drug deal. I sat up immediately and said, "Where are you?"

"By some railroad tracks and one of these niggas is acting like he has some kind of personal beef with me. But I will call you back later." At this time, he was good but didn't sound quite like himself. So I waited for another call, which wasn't until early the next morning, like 3:00 a.m. "Hey, Lesia, come get me out of here. These niggas are getting high and the same guy I told you about hit me in my face trying to be tuff in front of his boys and they keep asking me if I want to go for a ride to the park, which means "Are you ready to go for your last ride before we kill you' in slang." All of my brother's close friends and our family members drove to Pontiac and found out where he was. They got my brother out of the house and brought him back home.

I'm not sure what all took place when they got there or even how they found him. I was told not to ask any questions and I didn't.

Not long after that incident, Tony enrolled in Barber College so he could start cutting hair for a living. He can't go anywhere in Detroit without knowing someone or someone knowing him.

Our daddy was exactly the same wherever he went he knew lots of people also from east to west. As you see, children are the product of their parents in one way or another always. Both of them attend every person that they've ever known to pass away funeral. It can be rain, sleet, snow, or shine; Tony will not miss a funeral, because he is a friend to the end. So was our daddy. We all have a gang of friends. I guess it has something to do with the way we were raised. We moved all over the city before we were adults. Tonia, Tony, and myself are well liked by everyone we ever crossed paths with. (With the exception of how a few people felt about Tonia). Lol

IN THE GAME

It was 1988. I was living on Monterey down the street from Jeff, when I had a knock at the door. It was the UPS man—a gentleman that I attended high school with that I never got along with, Terrance was his name or what I thought was his name. He smiled when I came to the door. He said, "I just knew it was you when I saw the name, but can you believe that all these years I thought your name was Arethia Franklin?" So I said, "Well, Terrance, why did you think that?" He said, "My name is not Terrance. It's Terrick." Then I said, "Are you serious? So we both really never knew each other's names. That's messed up," and we shared a laugh. Then he said, "Do you live here by yourself?" I said, "Yes, just me and my son." I had no plan of becoming nothing but friends with him, so it was not his business that Court lived there also. Then Terrick leaned in really close to me and whispered, "Stop signing for these packages. They are watching you and your house." I thanked him, and he said, "Is it okay for me to have your number?" I said, "You sure can." I gave him my number, then he left me with the package.

The package contained over ten kilos of cocaine that I allowed to come to my house to make a quick one thousand dollars once a month for a while, like a fool. Back then, it seemed like a lot of money, but I never thought of what would have happened if I had gotten caught signing for all that dope. If I was as smart as I thought I was, I should have been charging them one thousand dollars per kilo instead even though that amount still wasn't enough to lose my son and my freedom. I was creeping with a guy names Brock around this time. We had a thing going on, but he had a main woman already.

During this time, I would have been considered to be his cold piece (that means the one who sits around and waits for another woman's man to come keep her warm whenever he could). But in my case, he was paying all my bills, keeping the refrigerator filled with food, giving me money for any needs my son may have, keeping my hair and nails done when needed, riding good in a different rental car every week, supplying me with all my other personal needs and plenty of money in the bank. A sister really couldn't complain. (You think?)

Brock would come to my house around ten every morning to order breakfast for the entire household from Lil's Grill, which was everybody's favorite hood spot to eat. After he ate, he would cook up, cut up, and bag his dope for the day and be on his way after he asked if there was anything I needed until his return. Now I had the day to do as I please. I did a lot of shopping, riding out, and just having a good time enjoying life. When nightfall hit, I would get a call from Brock letting me know he would meet me back at the house. We would eat dinner together then have a drink of cognac and watch a movie or something. We very rarely had sex. Our relationship was a real friendship, not just based around sex. Brock was a sweetheart, so I could never have mistreated him. He spent more time with me than his main woman daily. I loved him and he loved me. We just were good with what we had at the time.

After Tony and Brock reconciled their differences, about the money coming up short a few month prior, they began hanging out together again, they were both shot at a local strip club by a jealous boyfriend of one of the strippers. Brock was hit in very critical places and just laid in the middle of seven mile until the ambulance came. But Tony was able to drive himself to the ER once inside the hospital he collapsed at the counter. They both survived their injuries, but Brock's were much more serious than my brother's. Tony came home almost a month before Brock was released. We put together a welcome-home party for Brock and a happy-you're-better party for Tony at a local nightclub when some stray guys that no one knew came in and started some shit with Brock's younger brother. All hell broke loose with the ending result being his brother's ear got sliced off with a broken champagne bottle.

The club was destroyed, many people were injured, but no one lost their life out of our group of friends. The following morning, while watching the news, I overheard that a little girl was shot and killed while trying to escape bullets being fired into her home hours after the incident at the club. We later found out that our friends were involved in it and were all being hauled into jail by the police. Brock was charged with the murder even though I know for a fact he did not fire the gun that killed the little girl.

He is now serving natural life without the possibility of parole for being at the wrong place at the wrong time. Years later, I went for a visit to see him, and he expressed to me that he felt, yes, he should have done time for not thinking clearly and for just being there, but after almost serving twenty years at the time of my last visit, he felt that he should not have to spend the rest of his life in prison for a murder he didn't commit.

I feel so sorry for him because I could have possibly prevented this from happening, but I was too afraid for me and my sons life if I had told what I really knew about the case at the time. I wrote and received letters from him off and on over the years. I have been unable to look at him face-to-face due to my dishonesty along with the lack of trust I displayed to him. As a special friend, I let him down big time.

I'm sorry, Brock. I pray daily for your freedom.

Being a Woman

It didn't take long for me to figure out the drug world was not for me. You lose too many people you love either to jail or death, and you find out that *money* is truly the root of all evil. I made up all kinds of excuses of why Terrick could not come to my house while things were unraveling with Brock. We just met up outside of my home from time to time someplace. After the trial was over, I was upfront with him about it all. He understood. Our first few dates Terrick took me to very intimate and special places to him, by the water for a picnic, his favorite place to just think, or taking a quiet walk in the park, holding hands and enjoying nature. Terrick was unlike any other guy I had ever dated. He was not a street guy. He was involved in church, was raised a Muslim, loved family, and respected women and people in general. Terrick was more like Jeff than anyone else.

I've tried the rest, now let's try something different, I thought. We spent all our time together. I moved from the hood to an apartment further west. It was a one-bedroom apartment for my son and me. Most of all, no roommates ever again. My best friend got an apartment of her own within a mile from mine. We stopped seeing much of each other then, even though we lived very close to one another. I guess it was time to grow up and start our own lives. Terry didn't live with me during my first year of stay, but he was there visiting every day. We found out I was pregnant, so we had to move together to a bigger place. It was a two-bedroom flat, which was fine since we found out it was another boy, so JP and his new brother could share a room for a while. Terry was still working for UPS, so we were doing well financially until we had the baby, then I planned on returning to the workforce myself.

During my seventh month of pregnancy, I received a call around midnight from my brother's girlfriend, saying, "Lesia, I know it's late, but please wake up." I said, "What's wrong?" She said, "Your mama has been hit by a car, you need to go to the hospital."

I sat straight up in disbelief I had to get my thoughts together. Then said, "Okay, what hospital is she in?" She told me, and I said okay and hung up the phone. Mama was hit by a drunk driver, and it's a good thing that Mama was also drunk when the drunk driver hit her. It's what the doctors said saved her life.

When we arrived at Henry Ford Hospital she had been transferred to Southwest Detroit Hospital due to the fact she had no health insurance. Mama suffered a serious head injury. All of our friends in the neighborhood witnessed the accident they told us that she flew as high as the corner store rooftop then landed on the hood of the car because the woman hit the brakes after she hit her. She must have awaken from the sound of my mother's body against the car but she was up in the air by then. Before she came crashing down through the windshield onto the woman's lap. Mama needed over 100 stitches and staples in her head she had permanent brain damage. From the air getting into her skull after all the moving from one hospital to the next played a part also. My mother stayed in the hospital for a few months before she was released. When she came home, she was in a full-body cast. Every bone in her body was broken except for her baby finger. She required twenty-four-hour care. Mama had a long road to full recovery. Plus, she had one hell of a lawsuit with AAA auto insurance company.

I helped as much as I could with caring for Mama until I had the baby, who came in October of 1989. We named him Ramon. He was a big one for a woman only weighing 120 pounds and four feet eleven inches tall to deliver. I pushed out seven pounds eight ounces. I was a stay-home mother for a year before I returned to work. After a while, I decided I wanted to become a nurse. I received my certification, and then I began classes at the School of Licensed Practical Nursing. I only completed a year and a half before my mother became ill. She was diagnosed with a disease called lupus.

Lupus is an autoimmune deficiency disease that causes your immune system to attack itself. Instead of your immune system fighting off only bad antibodies, it fights off the good ones also. Trauma to the body usually triggers this disease.

Most of all stress does as well. When Mama was hit by the drunk driver, she began showing symptoms of lupus. Mama won her lawsuit. She received over a million dollars. We were all so happy for her. Mama gave us all a generous amount but not as much as we expected either. We understood later why she did this. Her plans were to save some for the future. But her doctors' bills took most of it. Dalvin, the buster-ass nigga she was with at the time, wanted to get married all of a sudden now that she has all this money. They have been together for over a decade and marriage never entered his thoughts. But Mama fell for the okeydoke and married the ass wipe.

Well, this knocked our black butts out of the picture regarding our future with the money. She furnished their place with very nice things, bought him a car and jewelry. She kept stacks of her money in his pockets. He no longer wanted us around. The isolation got worse over the last two years of her life. Then our children were no longer welcome to come whenever we came for a visit. They were tearing up things in their house, or Mama's head was always hurting. It's sad to know that our children only have memories of their grandmother as being a very mean person. We all had no idea at the time that her lupus was attacking her brain; therefore, she could have indeed been suffering with migraine headaches.

Most of the bullshit after the money came into play was from that nigga of hers. I was at the hospital every day until my mother passed. I learned as much as I could about the disease lupus. I did not handle her death well at all. In my mind, I envisioned what she would have been like as an old woman. Instead my mother left me at the early age of forty-seven. Her life should have just been beginning. After her death, we had to handle things that we were unprepared for, such as planning a funeral service, purchasing a headstone, and selecting a casket to bury our mother in. What in the world is happening? My head is spinning in circles. Mama knew she was dying but kept it to herself to ensure we would still treat her the same as usual. Her home-going service was beautiful. The church was packed. It helps when you know your loved one was loved by so many.

Dalvin allowed my siblings and me to do as we pleased for our mother's home going, so I do thank him for that.

Mama and I were the same and yet so different in many ways:

We both were very smart, intelligent young ladies that graduated from high school at the age of sixteen and a half: She graduated from Central, I attended Central until the 12 grade but took my GED in one day to be hired at BC/BS.

Sucked our thumbs as kids—she stopped at seventeen I never stopped.

Lived on Monterey as teenagers—but I moved back on Monterey as an adult.

Didn't have a good relationship with our mother—but I developed one with my mama as I got older.

We both had a child at the age of twenty—she had a child already at eighteen and she had me at the the age of twenty. And I also had my first child at twenty.

Didn't love the right man that loved us the most—we both learned later in life that we let the good ones get away.

Fell in love with the jailbird—we both were madly in love with the guy that caused us many problems and worries.

Showed true commitment to a drug addicted man—had no limits to what we would do

Slept with another woman's man—this is something that she did on a few occasions and I did only once to my knowledge.

Worked at BC/BS—mama worked for them for over ten years but I didn't make it to one hundred days.

Got beaten in head with an object—mama got hit with a pipe & I got hit with a bottle.

Both of us were thrown out at the hospital—mama at Detroit Memorial Hospital and I at Holy Cross.

Suffered from brain damage—mama's lupus attacked her brain and I suffered from central nervous system issues on the left side of my brain.

Felt our mother chose men over us—mama felt granny chose her husband over her and I felt my mama chose all her men over me.

Experienced a horrible abortion & miscarriage—mama was forced to have an abortion and I chose to have one. Mama had a miscarriage in her twenties as a women and I was a twelve year old child.

Molested by a family member—mama told family members but nothing was ever done about it, and I told no one about the first person because of what my mama said happen when she told. I just recently remembered who the second person was.

Diagnosed with lupus—mama was diagnosed after her accident when she was forty—two years old but we never knew until two months before she passed away at forty—seven years and I was diagnosed when I was thirty-four years old and still battle with the disease today at forty—seven years old.

Loved to dance—Ballroom dancing with my father is how they began their relationship as dance partners at The Grayston and I learned to ballroom dance from my daddy when I was ten years old.

Genuinely loved people—We both have lots of friends

Really loved our family—Family is all we have is what she taught me and this is what I installed in my children.

Mama really loved Terrick right from the start she felt he would be wonderful husband and a great father to my sons. So I stuck it out with him. We shared a nice life together I was happy to be a mother and his partner.

My First Marriage

Terrick and I decided to get married before my mother passed away. We drove to Ohio and had a courthouse marriage. It was held in the hallway of the courthouse in an isolated corner with Terrick and me and a reverend for about a five minutes ceremony and it was over. When we left Ohio, I felt like nothing happened. I expected a feeling of some sort. But it was nothing, except we were married. Mrs.Terrick Griffin. I wanted to live a different life, have my children grow up in a nice interracial neighborhood and go to the best schools, be a PTA parent, a good wife and mother, and just live the family lifestyle I never had.

We moved to our first single home in a far eastside upscale neighborhood, which was a really nice home, and I loved it. Much to my surprise, I really did. My neighbors were the best. Everyone was caring and concerned. I never had to worry about my home being broken into like I did in the hood or my children getting shot on their way to or back from school as I did. After five years, we had another baby, and it was the last one. It was another boy, seven pounds even. Lil Terrick Jr. was born in 1994. This delivery was life threatening. I suffered from placenta previa, which means the placenta detached and could have killed our baby.

After the baby was born, I was advised by the doctors that it would be in my best interest not to have any more children. We made the appointment to have my tubes tied after a few months. Things seemed to have gotten better between Terrick and me. We were back in love again until the summer came around. My sister was turning thirty years old that August. We had been spending a lot of time together, when I noticed a big weight loss from June to August. I asked my sister what size she wore since my plans were to get her an outfit for her birthday. She told me a size 9/10 in July, but by her birthday, she was wearing a size 5/6. "WTF is up, Tonia? Why have you lost so much weight?" She replied, "Girl, I don't know." I asked her to go to the doctors and be checked out. She agreed but never made an appointment.

Her youngest daughter Whitney was now one year and four months old. She had been in the hospital for the first eight months of her life from when Tonia began showing the early stages of lupus like our mother had. Tonia suffered a stroke and heart attack at the same time, was hospitalized for five months, and died that January. This tore my heart up. Inside, I really did not think I would be able to survive this episode. Losing my mother was a big enough pill to swallow.

Now you want me to handle losing my first best friend, it's been only three years Lord! This is when I found out how strong of a woman I really was.

Breathe through it; take it one day at a time, Lesia. God only puts on you what you can handle. These were my thoughts, and they helped me get by. Terrick was the one who thought of the idea of getting all five of the kids and raising them as our own. He was a wonderful man to even think of opening up our lives to such a big responsibility, and I love him for that even to this day. Thank you, Terrick, for being a real man at the most important time of my life. We took them all and became their guardian. All was well until I began neglecting my husband totally, and my mind was just wrapped up in the loss of my sister and caring for all eight of the children.

Terrick lost his mind one day. After a long day at work, he walked in the door and said, "Can I talk to you for a moment?" I said, "Yes." He said, "Lesia, do you realize that we have not had sex in months?" I replied, "And?" He said, "What do you mean 'And'?" I said, "Who do you think would be thinking about having sex when they have just lost their mother and sister, plus on top of that inherited five more children that constantly remind me of both of them?" He said, "What about your husband?" I said, "You just have to understand." Terrick took his fist and knocked on my forehead as if he was knocking on a door and yelled, "You need to snap out of this. Are you fucking brain-dead?"

I went ballistic and ran straight to the cordless phone, locked myself up in the bathroom, and called the police as if he had just beat the shit out of me. The police came. Once they saw I was only 4'11" and Terry was 6'2", they did not ask any questions. They just took him to jail for the night. All the children were upset with me because I was truly wrong for calling the police. But I think I needed someone to be angry with, and he was the one. I went to pick him up the following morning, and things were never the same between us from that point on. We separated shortly after and went our own way.

Once Terrick left, I decided to return to work as a private nurse. I enjoyed working with the elderly and knowing I was helping someone. Terrick and I tried to reunite by going on dates and spending time together, but we could not work it out. Things were tense for a while between us. But eventually, we were able to become friends, and we agreed to raise our children together. Terrick and I were still married for three years before we divorced in 1999. We shared custody of the children. Terry remarried the same year we divorced. He met someone and had another child—his only daughter. The children and I remained in the house until Mook came home from prison.

A Big Blow to the Head

I began working for the Michigan Rehabilitation Institute for a doctor in a small office downtown. It was a nice environment. The people I worked with were very nice, and the doctor was handsome as hell. I had somewhat of a small crush on him, but I kept this to myself. I worked both the front and back end of the office when needed. The doctor was very friendly to his employees. He would purchase lunch for us at least three times a week or take us all out to very fine restaurants whenever we didn't have a heavy workflow for the day.

After working there for over a year, we were all comfortable with one another, but I never talked about my personal life, and boy, did they want to know what was going on with me. I began writing letters to Mook once Terrick and I ended. He told me that he had a couple of more years left to serve in prison, so this just gave me something to do as a time passer. He wrote me some of the sexiest poems, and his letters just made me so wet that it was so easy for me to take care of myself sexually. And let's not forget the phone conversations; they were off-the-hook nasty.

Well, this was my first time dealing with a man in prison, I had no idea that there were guys in prison that are so fucking talented that he could make a living selling greeting cards and become multimillionaires. But instead they may have done some old off-the-wall dumb shit that caused them to be placed in prison. Plus they order books & magazines on how to treat a woman. Whatever the reason was Mook said what I needed to hear that kept me motivated at the time. And he wrote me what I needed to read. I could not wait for these two years to pass so we could make it all a reality.

Back to the office—all of a sudden, out of the blue, I began receiving flowers, cards, candies, balloons, big bears, and other gifts from an anonymous person for about two to three months without this person revealing himself. I really believed Mook was having them sent to me all along until one evening on a Saturday, the doctor asked all the ladies in the office if we would like to go out for a few drinks—on his expense of course. As always, I was the only person to refuse the offer in the office because, I was the only one that had eight children at home waiting on my return.

All the girls were begging me to come. "Just for a little while," they said. I was contemplating the offer all the way to my car as we were leaving for the day, then I thought to myself, Damn, girl, you haven't been anywhere outside of work and home for about a year now. You should go. Before they all pulled off, the doctor came to my car and said, "So we're just not good enough for Ms. Arlesia to hang out with for a few drinks huh?" I replied, "No, it's not that. I have eight children at home waiting for me to come cook dinner." He yelled, "Eight children? You are playing, right?" I became immediately pissed and said, "Why would I play about something like that?"

"You never told me that you had eight children, Arlesia." I replied, "I didn't have to." My blood pressure was boiling out of anger. Also that was my first time ever revealing my personal business to anyone. He said with a smile, "I'm sorry. I didn't mean anything by it when I yelled like that, but what if we go to your house and drop off something for them to eat first then will you go out with us?" I sat there for a moment to think about it and gave in and said, "Okay. That will work. But I will take

them something for dinner then just meet you all there shortly." He said, "That's fine," then gave me the address to the locations, and we went our separate ways.

I stopped by a fast-food chain close to the house, took it home, and made sure everything was all right at the house and the kids were all okay. I told the oldest, Jamell, where I was going then called my neighbor to ask her to keep an eye on the house because I was going out for a while. Changed my clothes, put on a little makeup and perfume, and headed back out the door. As I was driving, Mook called. I don't know why, but I lied to him and said I was on my way home. I had a headache and was going to take some Tylenol, shower, and go to bed for the night. He told me to get some rest, and he hoped I felt better. He would talk to me the next day. We said our I-love-yous and hung up the phone.

I continued to drive to the location. When I pulled up, I couldn't believe how lovely it was. Off the water, there was a pleasant breeze blowing as we all sat on the deck. We ate, laughed, and drunk up a couple of bottles of Merlot. The food was delicious, and so was the wine. I was having such a blast I lost track of time. I looked at my watch; it was close to midnight. We had been drinking for almost five hours. I was tipsy, so I stopped my drinks from coming to try and sober up a bit. Then to my surprise, the doctor pulls out some weed and asked if anyone wanted to smoke. I wasn't a weed smoker, so I refused, but the other girls took him up on the offer. I was thinking, Dum-dums, this is still your boss. But they were all adults, so it was not my problem.

The night ended around 2:00 a.m., and we all headed to our cars. The doctor walked me to my car and said, "I had a wonderful time, and I am so happy you decided to attend. I love the way you smile, and I found out tonight that you really like Merlot. So I will keep some available at all times from now on for you." He opened my door and said, "Keep smiling, I love it." He closed my door and bid me farewell. As I drove away, I noticed that this man was flirting with me. Remember, he is your boss, girl, and I shook the thought out of my head.

Back to work on Monday, as usual, everyone was still talking about our outing when the door opened, and it was another delivery, but it's a box wrapped all pretty addressed to me from my secret admirer. I opened it, and it's a bottle of Merlot with a card of a big smile on it. I looked around for the doctor, but he was nowhere in sight. My heart stopped for a second, then I thought this secret admirer can't be him. Now I'm feeling all uneasy. I put the wine in my locker and never mentioned it to any of the girls. As I was leaving for the day, the doctor calls me in his office.

I go inside. He was sitting at his desk and said, "You like your gift?" I answered, "Yes, I did, thank you."

"I bought it for you because you seem like you need something to help you relax." I answered, "I have someone to help me relax." Then he said, "Really?" and I said, "Yes, really."

I turned around and walked out of his office. Before the door closed, he said, "Have a good evening, Arlesia." I replied, "You do the same, Doctor." I got home, prepared dinner, helped those who needed help with homework, talked to Mook, then took a bath, read a few pages to a novel, opened the bottle of wine and drunk a glass and went to sleep.

Wow! I woke up feeling refreshed. I did not know that a bath and a glass of wine before bed could make me sleep so well. Work was good that day. We were very busy. The doctor kept looking at me, smiling most of the day. After the last patient left, the doctor made a statement, "Ladies, a friend of mine is having a birthday party on Saturday. He asked me to bring you, ladies, if you want to go. But I need to know today so I can RSVP for all of us at the same time." We caught eye contact, and he said, "And you are going, Arlesia."

All eyes were on me. I looked, and before I knew it, everyone was all over me, talking about "Yeah, you seem so different since we went out last week. You're much more loose not so uptight. You even look better not always like you are ready to fight." I stepped back and said, "All right, I'll go." The doctor was like, "That's what's up. We're going to have a great time too. Oh, make sure you all dress up. It's a black-tie event. This is why I let you all know so soon." Everyone left, headed home. I turned on my radio, and my jam was on—"Secret Lovers." I blasted the radio, singing all the way home. I pulled up to my house, and the kids were waiting for me to come inside. They were all in the window and stuff.

I'm like, "What's up, yawl?" They asked, "Can we go to the drive-in tonight?" I was in such a good mood I said right away, "Yeah, that sounds good." I called Lori and asked if she wanted to join us. We packed up the van and stopped by the store for goodies. I had my bottle of wine, and we all went to the drive-in. As the children were all in front of the van in their chairs, Lori and I talked. I told her about the doctor and about the admirer to get her opinion if she thought it was all the doctor or was Mook sending the gifts. She said she thought it was Mook and the doctor just sent the wine. I wondered why he didn't sign the card that was attached like all the other things that came with a card. I rolled with what she said and threw the thoughts of it being the doctor out the window. We had a good time with our children watching the movie.

Back to work, a few days before the birthday party, and I was looking forward to going. My alarm rang on my phone. It read one year until Mook is released from prison. This was a message I programmed when he told me his release date. Instantly, a warm feeling came over my body. I knew I loved this man. I always had. I just hoped it was not going to be a long wait for nothing. I was just hoping he would come home and stay home. He had been back and forward in and out of jail since he was twelve years old. But this was his first time going to prison. This was all the way different from the county jails and much longer. Most of the girls went out to lunch that day. It was just me and another girl that stayed in the office for lunch.

The doctor was in his office having lunch I assumed. When he opened his office door and called my name, I got up and went to his office. He said, "Come inside and close the door." I stepped inside. He then said, "Have a seat please." I took a seat. He opened his drawer and pulled out an envelope and handed it to me. I could feel there was a card inside of it. I asked, "What is this, Doctor?" He said, "Your bonus." I opened it, and it was a gift card for Nordstrom's worth $500. "Go buy *yourself something nice to wear for the party and whatever else you want to do with the rest." My eyes began to swell with tears. He then said, "You are a wonderful person, and you deserve something nice for yourself sometimes, Arlesia." I thanked him and walked out of his office.*

I was quiet for the remainder of the afternoon. I finished my work and left for the day. Driving home, I put on the slow jam station and "Fairy Tales" by Anita Baker came on. As it played, I imagined myself riding on the back of a horse with the doctor and daydreaming of him sweeping me away into never-never land with his dreadlocks flowing to his shoulders, his shirt opened a few buttons revealing his chest muscles, me holding on to him tightly around his waist, feeling safe and secure. Boy, I was falling for the doctor. I drove straight to Summit Set Mall after work to find me something beautiful to wear to the event. I found the perfect fitting dress that revealed all my curves in every way. Now I had to find shoes to match. I finally found a pair along with jewelry to complete the outfit.

The day had finally come. I got my hair and nails done, also a birthday gift for the man of the hour before I returned home to bathe, moisturize my body with lotion, slipped into my new black thong and bra set, slide up my shimmering white sheer pantyhose, zipped up my new bad-ass all-white rhinestone-fitted sexy dress with silver accessories, sprayed on some Gucci perfume, put on my silver sling back sandals then grabbed my silver handbag off the shelf in my closet. It was so nice outside, I did not need a sweater. Pulled out the Cadillac and was on my way.

I parked in valet and pranced inside like I was the only woman there, placed the gift on the gift table. The doctor stood up as I entered the room. He raised his arm so I could see where he was sitting. I headed his way. Once I approached the table, he pulled my seat out for me to sit down. What a gentleman, I thought. He whispered in my ear, "Arlesia, you look beautiful." I replied, "Thank you, and you're looking very handsome yourself." He said, "Thank you." We gave each other a pleasant smile.

The event was located in one of the ballrooms at the Renaissance in downtown Detroit. This event was one of the classiest events I ever attended. The food was delicious, the band was great, and the drinks were flowing all night, also desserts. There was an ice sculpture of his friend's whose party it was. Along with gift bags for all the guests. The doctor and I danced several times, and I also danced with other men. It was a night to remember. I went to the ladies' room to freshen up after all the dancing then returned to the table when the doctor said, out of the blue, "Arlesia, did you ever find out who your secret admirer was?" I answered, "No, as a matter of fact, I haven't." He smiled, then said, "I'm your secret admirer." I turned blue in the face. It was like I couldn't breathe. Just when I stopped thinking it, he said this. All my coworkers were looking at me with their mouths wide open in shock like I was. I stood up and ran out of the room.

I have never been so embarrassed in my life. The doctor ran behind me. I could hear him calling my name, "Arlesia, wait. Please wait. Why are you running away?" I was crying and saying, "Because why would you say something like that in front of all my coworkers?" He said, "They all needed to know because I couldn't hold it anymore. I love you, Arlesia. I don't know what it is, but you're just so different from any other woman I have met. You're so genuine and kind."

"But I'm married," I said. He said, "But you like me too." I didn't know what to say. I was speechless. Then he shocked the hell out of me and said, "He won't be home for another year. Anything can happen in a year." My eyes got big, and I said, "How do you know that?"

"Because I did a background check on you. I found out your sister died and you took her kids. That's how you have eight children. I also found out you are not married for real. So why are you lying? I like you so much, I have to have you. Would you rather have a jailbird or a doctor?"

I threw up my hands and told him, "This is too much. I have to go. I will talk to you later. I need to go now."

I got in my car once the valet pulled up and pulled off.

Thank God it was Sunday, so I didn't have to look at him that day. I woke all the kids up for church. We were going to the Catholic Church that one of my patients attended. After mass, we were back home before 10:00 a.m. We ate breakfast and lay around the house all day until around 3:00 p.m. when the boys asked if they could go to the skating rink. This sounded like a good idea. I needed to get out and do something to keep my mind occupied. I had not skated in a while, so I was a little rusty on the floor, but the kids were pretty good skaters. We enjoyed our time together, so this made my day. We ate dinner at the rink, so everyone took their baths and got ready for bed once we returned home. Mook called. We talked for a short while, and I got in the bed.

I sat up in bed most of the night. I was so emotionally wrecked. I made up my mind that I wasn't going into work the next day before I even got home. My alarm went off at 7:00 a.m., so I called the answering service to call off for the day. Got the kids ready for school, dropped them off, and stayed in bed all day.

I wanted Mook to call me so bad, but he never called during the day, only after I got off work. So I just took in a few talk shows and soaps, cooked dinner early, took the dog for a walk, and sat at the park for a while before it was time to pick the kids back up from school. It was a long day since I was so used to going to work. I was surprised the doctor did not call me, I must admit, but he didn't. He knew I was livid with his ass for how he did what he did.

Tuesday morning, I went in to work. Everyone was sort of distant with me that day, which was fine. I needed the space. I worked as I always did, went to my car to eat my lunch, returned to the office, completed my day, and headed home. The doctor said only what he had to say to me, and I did the same. This went on for the remainder of the week. Until Friday—I received another package. It was a gift basket full of I'm sorry things inside, attached with a card stating how sorry he was for coming off like he did. He should have taken another approach to the situation and so on and so on. After I opened it, I put it in my locker and continued to work. It was time to punch out, and the doctor came over to me and asked that I come to his office before I leave for the day. I walked to his office, and he said, "I am so sorry, Arlesia. It will never happen again, I promise you." I said okay and walked to punch out and left.

The tension between the doctor and I got better after about a week. Before long, things were back to normal. He stopped sending gifts, and I was kind of upset that he did. Mook would be home in about ten months when the doctor asked if we all wanted to join him for drinks at a Jamaican club. The doctor was Jamaican. I accepted but had to go home first to take care of my kids, of course changed into some jeans, and headed out. Once inside the club, it hit me like a brick. The marijuana smell was so strong but smelled good. The music was smooth.

I liked the scenery; it was nice. All the guys were all so cool, the ladies danced the night away, and the reggae music was very sensual it made you want to move in a sexy swaying type of way.

We had a ball tonight. Everybody was high, even me, off the marijuana. I took a few puffs while we were there. It was still early, so the doctor asked if we wanted to come see his house, but a couple of his friends were coming also if we didn't mind. We all were partying together most of the night already and they all appeared to gentlemen, so we didn't mind. When I pulled up to his home, I was in awe. It was so big and beautiful. I loved his landscape, I could not believe my eyes. Whoever decorated his home had really good taste. I liked everything in his house. It was all in the right places also. I glanced at the doctor to see if he was watching, and of course he was. He opened his home to us and told us to make ourselves comfortable, so I did. I found a very comfortable chaise lounge chair to lay in, and this was where I was during my visit.

We all laughed and talked. We even played a few games. It was a good old time. I called to check on the kids; they were good. Most were asleep. The older ones were watching movies. So I continued on with my good time. I believe I drank a whole bottle of wine by myself. Now good and high, we decided to play truth or dare. Once my turn came around, I asked, "This is for all the ladies from work. Truth or dare?" They all said truth. I asked, "Is it true that all of you hoes like the doctor?" They said,

"Hell yeah, the doctor is fine and sexy as fuck." The doctor said, "What, you got to be kidding me?" Then one of the girls said, "But the doctor has his eyes elsewhere, right, Doc?" He then said, "You got that right. She will be here in about five minutes." I was messed up just knowing he was talking about me until he said the five minutes shit.

I said nothing. I continued to lay across the chaise lounge chair and be cool. Five minutes, ten minutes, and one hour went by. No one came. So what was he talking about? Was he just playing or playing me to get a response? I knew I liked the doctor, but Mook was coming home soon. Before we knew it, 3:00 a.m. hit. A few people began to leave. A few stayed. The doctor told us we could if we wanted to. I was high, so I wasn't driving. I called to let Jamell know where I was. He had my number if he needed me. I dozed off and was awakened to someone rubbing my feet. It felt so good. I have not been touched by a man in close to three years. I was horny as hell, and this man was the perfect one to give some cookies and milk to. So I laid there and enjoyed the massage that I needed so much. It wasn't rushed he took his time with me rubbing me slow and gentle from my feet to my shoulders. I loved every moment of this. My entire was relaxed before he said, "How does that feel Arlesia"? I said, "Oh so good Doc and much needed".

"Where is everybody, Doc?" He told me no one was there but me and him. He got up walked to his stereo to put on some music and began male dancing to a Jamaican song. His body was tight from working out daily. He ate healthy. He always smelled so good from the oils he wore. I was turned on. He began to suck my toes while he was rubbing my legs softly. His hands were getting closer and closer to my pussy as he rubbed between my legs, up my thighs. I never resisted. I opened them more and more the higher he got until my legs were completely opened. He brushed his hands across the zipper of my jeans and unzipped them. He pulled his body up over me and slid down to my stomach and began putting his tongue inside my navel, swirling it around and around, then down to the top of my panty line. He lifted me up to take off my jeans and then my panties with his teeth.

Once my panties were off, he proceeded to lick all over my stomach and between my thighs. I was dying inside for him to suck my clit.

I could feel my juices beginning to pour over when he started sucking my pussy so soft and with the right amount of pressure. He pulled back with my clit between his teeth but not hurting me but allowing my orgasm to spill inside his mouth and all over his chin. I closed my eyes as a tear ran down my cheek. I was so excited. This man knew exactly what he was doing. He lifted my ass up and turned me over on my stomach then pulled me back towards him as he put his tongue in my ass and began to suck my ass clit that no other woman that I know has. Yes. I have asked my girlfriends. I'm Original.

This was something new for me, but I liked it. He told me to get up on my knee so he could hit it from the back. I paused and asked, "Hit what?" He said, "That pussy." Just checking and I obeyed his request. He put his dick inside of my pussy with minimal pressure as possible my pussy was so tight he whispered Damn baby you haven't had this pussy hit in a minute I see. Pumping trying to get deep inside of me as slow as he could to avoid hurting himself once he was completely inside me he began massaging the insides of my soul. He was so gentle in every stroke I just came over and over again. My legs began to shake uncontrollably the feeling was so intense. I wanted it to never stop.

Doc, you are the bomb, baby, I was thinking to myself. He slowed down, pulled out, told me to turn around, and said, "Now Ride this Dick, baby." I got down on it and went to work. Recapturing the great feeling that was just given to me by this man. I rode it nice and slow so he could feel inch of my pussy. I made sure his dick hit all the walls from the front to back. Pussy juice was all over his dick. He moaned and groaned as I allowed his big dick to go in and out of me. It was soaked and wet all over his chaise. He said, "Let's go up to my room. I have something else for you," he said. I followed him to his bedroom. As we came to the door of his room, he swept me off my feet and held me with both hands like we were just married, and he carried me over the threshold.

Since this was something that I had never done before, I said not a word. He placed me on his bed with care then lit a candle that was on the nightstand. The candle was scented with a very nice fragrance as it burned while the doctor licked my entire body.

Afterward, he rubbed me down with massage oil, and he gave a great massage. His hands were so strong. I wanted him back inside of me bad, but he made me wait for it. He whispered, "Tonight belongs to you, Ms. Arlesia. It's time someone took care of you for a change. One minute." He walked away, and I heard water coming from the bathroom attached to his bedroom. He held out his hand for me to take. I did, following him with anticipation of what's next. The shower door was opened for me to enter. Once inside, I heard a vibrating sound. He said, "I bought this just for you.

He was holding a flesh colored vibrator that had with bunny ears on the lower portion close to the shaft. The package is on the counter over there." I looked over to the sink to see packaging of some sort lying on the countertop. "It goes in all kinds of positions. Let me show you how it feels." So he began to rub it over my breast and clip my nipples between the ears while the water was running over my entire body. "Relax," he said. I took a deep breath. He slowly dropped to his knees and began to suck my pussy. Inside of me, he went with the vibrator. I leaned against the wall. Mirrors were everywhere, so he could see my every expression.

This man was very experienced with women. He could see that it felt so good to me and that he was in total control of the situation, I allowed him to have his way with me. Just as long as he didn't touch my asshole, Other than that I was all right with whatever. My legs began to shake vigorously as I came for the doctor once more. He stepped out of the shower for a moment and came back with a shower chair and a big white towel. He laid the towel across the chair and told me to lay over the towel but allow my arms to touch the floor and keep my ass up in the air so he could get all pussy.

He also said he wanted the cold water to beat at my pussy from the back so my clit would freeze before he let me come again. He pulled the shower sprayer down and directed to my pussy, set the massager to the soft sprayer level first at a warm temperature, then to a firmer spray level at a cool temperature until I began to moan, to the firmest spray level at the cold temperature he aimed the sprayer straight for my clit until it got so hard I was begging for him to stop. It was intense, cold, uncontrolled, and a complete turn on for me. The doctor spoke at a low voice saying take it baby, take it.

He never put his dick inside of me, and I released the creamiest and thickest orgasm I had ever had. It oozed out slowly then down my thigh. The doctor then began to suck my pussy before I sprayed all over the shower floor. This was my first multiple orgasm. It was one to remember. I held my pussy with my hands so tightly between my legs because the feeling just kept going and going and going. When I opened my eyes to look at him, he had his dick in his hands with so much nut dripping from it. He was hard then, a motherfucker with a smile so big over his face. I asked him, "Where did you learn that?" He replied, "From my homeland." We both cleaned up and went back into his bedroom to lie across his bed. I said, "Doctor, that was wonderful, much needed and worth it. You know it's been a long time coming, but your sexy ass is hard to resist especially with me having to see you almost every day. But you know Mook is coming home soon, so this can't happen ever again." As I lay on his chest in his bed, I believe his heart stopped for a second. He said nothing.

Finally the doctor spoke. He said, "So you tell me you never made love like this before, you tell me that you never had multiple orgasms before, you tell me your man is in prison, and you have along for some time now, but then you also tell me that this can never happen again." He yelled, "Woman! What in the fuck are you going through?

After how we just made each other feel, you don't want it again?" I replied, "It was just sex. Something we both needed at the time, but strings don't have to be attached behind it." The doctor got up from his bed and looked angry. He paced the floor for a while before saying, "Yeah okay, just sex, okay. You want something to eat or drink? I'm *going to the kitchen for some water." I replied, "Yes, I can use a bottle of water." He left the bedroom. I wasn't sure what to think at this point. He returned with my water in hand, gave it to me while looking in my eyes in a cold type of way, and shook his head while smiling. "You are something different, lady," the doctor said. He got back in the bed, put his hand behind his head, and lay on his pillow. Before long, we were both asleep.*

We woke up around 11:00 a.m. He cooked breakfast for me. He ate then he walked me to my car, but the doctor was not the same. He appeared to be very sad or disappointed. I said, "Thanks for a wonderful time." He said, "The same here, Ms. Arlesia." Then I said, "I will see you at the office on Monday, Doc," and I drove off. While driving, I was thinking all the way home. Why did I have to have sex with him? I should have gone home when everyone else was leaving. Did I get drunk on purpose just to stay? My emotions were all over the place. If I am really in love with Mook, it would not have happened. Oh my god, I blew it. I really did. With Mook and the doctor, I'm acting just like a man fucking without feelings of love.

Once I made it home, I allowed my day to continue as usual. I asked the kids if they wanted to do something fun that day. Of course they always said yes, so we planned a picnic and a day at the beach. I called up my girl Lori, asked her to join us at the beach with her children, and we had a very good time. The doctor called me a few times throughout the day to keep reminding me of how much of a wonderful time he shared with me and how he wanted to do it all over again.

This went on all day Sunday. Also he kept repeating how much more he could do for me, how he could put me in a happier and much better situation than I was currently involved in. Blah, blah, blah is what it sounded like to me. My heart belonged to Mook, so, buddy, take a backseat. By Monday morning, I decided not to return to work because I knew things were going to be awkward behind the whole sex event. So I called in on Monday, then also Tuesday. I went to the temporary agency that I used to work for requesting an assignment. There was an opening beginning the following Monday. I took it and didn't return to the office again.

Doc called my cell repeatedly, leaving message after message. When finally he called my home, one of the children answered and called my name to come to the phone. I picked up the upstairs phone. "Hello," I said. "So this is how we're going to handle this, Arlesia?" said the doctor. "Handle what?" I replied. "You know exactly what I'm talking about. You're just going to quit on me, no call nothing." I said, "Doc, this is for the best. Things went too far, and it's all my fault. I can't handle two situations at one time, so I decided just to stick with my first situation." He said, "So you're choosing to wait for him huh? "I said, "Yes I have." There was a moment of silence then the doctor said, "Well, that's all you had to say." I said, "Well I believe I did in plain English at your house." Then the doctor asked, "So let's just go out for a drink. Everything is cool. We can still be friends, right?"

I said, "Yes, we're still friends, but I have to pass on the drink this time."

"But why?" he said.

"I have a new job that I start tomorrow, so I need my rest, and I don't drink during the week."

"Well, let me pick you up to go for a short ride down Jefferson along the shoreline so we can just talk this over and come to an understanding because you're making me feel like I did something wrong to you and this was not my intention," Doc said. I paused for a moment before he switched up and yelled so loud, "Look, bitch, either you come outside or I'm coming inside. Look out your window." He was parked in front of my house in his BMW. I could not believe he was at my home and didn't want any harm to come toward my children at all. My heart dropped inside of me. Then I said, "Okay, give me a minute."

I called my oldest nephew, Jamell, to come see what car I was leaving in and told him to write down the license plate number. I walked out, got in the car, and we drove away down Three Mile to Jefferson Avenue. I sat quietly. The doctor began the conversation. "Hey, I don't usually get that way, but damn, baby, you have just changed overnight for no reason at all." I just sat back and listened to him talk. "The part that trips me out the most is that you would rather wait for a nigga that's been in and out of prison over being with me, a doctor. Are you crazy or something?" he said. "Not at all," I replied. "Well, what's the reason you don't want to be with me?"

"Because I love Mook and always have. What happened with us was not supposed to happen, but it did. It was just a one night stand. You're nice, handsome, and all of that, but you can get anyone else, Doc, and you know it." You did the background check found out I wasn't really married then decided Arlesia has been by herself for a good while I know she is lonely, horney, desperate or whatever you thought. Plus you knew all the ladies at the office was digging you. But I must have appeared to be the weakest link. So you chose me Right? He yelled, "Hell No baby from the moment you interviewed I was liking you. Your smile is beautiful you light up a room with that alone. Your conversation is always interesting and your laugh is outrageous. I watch you walk in and leave daily. That ass is tight as fuck. I just want to make you my wife and take good care of you that's all I want you. You are insulting my intelligence, you know that? You're playing me like a man does women. You are not going to get away with it either!

He reached down in front of his seat and pulled up a 40 oz Colt 45 and backhanded me in the face so fast with it before I even knew it. All I saw were stars before my eyes, then I passed out from the blow to the head. Once I came to, I was in a room full of bright lights over me, and a lady was asking me questions about who did this to me. They told me I was thrown out at the ER door by a person driving a black BMW. It was all recorded on the monitoring system. I couldn't open my eyes; they were partially closed shut. The swelling was severe. The bottle didn't break; thank God I wasn't all cut up too. But the impact of the full bottle did major damage to my head and behind my eye.

I was most happy that I got in the car with this fool. There was no idea what he would have done to me or my children at my house. I began to panic right away once the thought crossed my mind. I needed to call my kids. I yelled for someone to come assist me. I called; they were all okay. I told them not to let anyone inside the house. I would call my neighbor to keep an eye on the house and to check on them. I would be home shortly. Before long, I heard a voice that I recognized. It was my brother, Tony. He was asking around, "Arlesia, where is she? I don't see her." I began waving my arms since I couldn't see him. All of a sudden, I heard "Damn, this motherfucker fucked you up. Where does that nigga live, sis?" I could feel a tear running down my face out of embarrassment of my brother seeing me like this, and I could feel the hurt in his voice about how bad I looked.

My brother knew I had been going out with the doctor, so I couldn't lie about who it was. Tony said, "He hangs out at the Jamaican club, right? He is Jamaican too with dreads. How tall is he, and what does he drive? Do you have a picture of him, Lesia? He is not getting away with this shit for sure." My head was pounding from the pain. I just wanted nothing but silence for now. They kept me for observation until the morning.

I called in to my new job to inform them that I was in the hospital and told them what had happened, so they got me a replacement for two weeks. Tony took me home and made me pack a few things so the children and I could stay at his home for a few days to help me out. The children didn't know what to do when they saw my face. They didn't ask any questions I believe the look on my brothers' face told them not to say a word. I stayed in the bedroom to avoid the children's stares.

I couldn't stand the thought of the kids seeing me that way. So during the night I called one of my male best friends to come pick me up. I left a note for my brother and his girlfriend so they would know where I was. I stayed a few days at my bestie's house to allow the swelling to go down. But all I really wanted was to be home in my own environment where I could be more comfortable. He refused for me to go back there until the police caught the doctor. He went to the store the next day and bought some Cognac to me relax and it did work. We drunk about a pint together before my friend for the first time expressed to me how he felt about me and about how much it hurt him to see me this way. I began to cry with the drinking it allowed me to show my feeling about what had happen as well. I expressed to him how much I missed my mother and sister, about how I feel alone all the time. About how I have tried to do the right thing by taking my sisters children as I would have hoped she would have done for me.

I cried about how no one even picks up the phone to ask if I needed a break from the kids for a few hours or even overnight. I worked all the time and wasn't allowing myself to have any time for myself and look where it got me once I finally decided to let my hair down and try to live a normal 31 year old woman's lifestyle I get beat with a bottle by a doctor, now I look like a monster. All because of a one night stand.

SEX—a very dangerous game to play with. He watched me closely as I talked, cried, drunk my cognac laying across his bed and before I knew it he kissed me on my cheek.

He said, you don't look like a monster Lesia you're still pretty before long you will be back to normal, that guy is a lame ass nigga for hitting you with a bottle. But when they catch his ass they will more than likely send him back to Jamaica where his ass needs to be or something. Don't worry about girl I will always be here for you.

I promised myself that I would appreciate a good man from that point on. I really never should have left Terrick. He was a good man, and so was Jeff, but I always thought there was something better than what I already had. Waiting for me across the street. I just had to walk across the street to see it, and look where it got me—absolutely nowhere. The grass is not always greener on the other side of the street. It just looks like that, something like a mirage. I never told my brother where the doctor lived or anything else about the doctor because it was my fault that this had to happen to me and no one else.

I played with his heart, and he could not accept my rejection of him. The doctor ended up losing his license and went to jail. The state picked up the case. He was charged with attempting to do great bodily harm.

They couldn't charge him with kidnapping because I didn't have to get in the car. I should've called the police while I was inside my home. Seeing him in the court room was weird now the doctor is a prisoner it's amazes me to know that your life can change in a split second. So never say never.

I could not believe I have been hit in the head by a man just like my mama did by the cab driver. This was a very big lesson learned for me. I will never judge a book by its cover. As my mama used to say, "Everything that glitters isn't gold." I allowed myself to be taken off guard because this man was a doctor, he was nice looking, he smelled good, drove a nice car, treated me nice, showered me with gifts, and played with my mind, and look where it got me—just a great big blow to the head.

My thoughts after the hit were shit I have been in love with a true street guy since I was 12 years old who never put his hands on me not even when I felt I deserved it. Because I had such a file mouth at times. But a so called—professional man who had so much to lose did something like this to me. I can't wait until my thug thistle comes home to me.

Still Down For Me

Yeah, that's right, the same old Mook from 1980. He had to serve some time in prison, but once he returned, the search was on for who else? His one and only Lesia! I do not know why, but I had a thing for thug ass nigga's, and Mook was definitely one from his head to his toes.

I was working in my brother's salon as a shampoo girl when he walked in went straight to my brother, his barber. They gave each other five and hugged, then Mook asked, "Where is Lesia?" Tony said, "My sister Lesia?" With laughter in his voice, Mook said, "Who else?" Tony replied, "Right behind you." He turned, and I kissed him right on his big juicy lips so passionately that the love for returned at the instants.

He held me tight with a loving hug for a very long time. I could feel all my old feelings for him resurfacing. We were together from that day on.

Fresh flowers were delivered to my job almost every week. If not flowers, it was balloons, or he took me on a shopping spree. He kept my hair and nails done whenever needed. He gave me his personal full body massages when I became tense. He refurnished my entire house and gave the children the best Christmases ever. They loved him as much as I did. We were one big happy family. No separation of "this is my father" or "not your father," Mook accepted all the children as his own—all eight of them—and no one could tell him different. It was really nice to have a man come in and bring the sunshine with him after all the sadness I had experienced over the past years. It was good to relax my mind, body, and soul for a change. I could finally allow someone else to handle the stress, and I could just fall back and look beautiful and be stress-free.

Mook knew what it took to keep a smile on his woman's face. This brother read the correct books while he was doing time, is all I can say.

He was just what I needed at this time of my life. It wasn't long before I was back in the same fire I jumped out of when I got with Terrick, holding drugs and guns, living the dangerous life for the quick dollar. Now a full-grown woman, I knew exactly what I was doing. I loved the rush of living on the edge; it was a part of my makeup, I guess. I was a product of the streets and wanted to get ahead as fast as possible.

I somewhat lost my mind. I began living a carefree lifestyle all over again. The children were not directly exposed to what was going on with me, but they were not fools. We were getting things that were expensive. They knew Mooch and I were not working. They knew these things were purchased with drug money.

"I had to take care of these kids by any means necessary" is what stayed on the mind constantly, and that's what I did. I had to be guarded by angels (Mama and sister) during this time because one day, I was home watching TV when the *Oprah Show* came on and mentioned if there was anyone interested in having their children enrolled in private schooling to call the number to enter into a contest. I called the number and entered into the contest that same day. Within a couple of weeks, I was contacted, and they informed me that our family was chosen.

I was so blessed to have seven out eight children enrolled into a Catholic school of my choice until they graduated from high school at an extremely discounted amount. I paid 25 % for every other three and four attended for free. Oprah paid 50% and the school waived the other 25% of the tuition cost. The only bad thing was that they all could not attend because the oldest was already in high school at the time. They had to be no older than twelve years old, so Jamell was the only one that didn't qualify.

If you don't mind I would love to introduce to you my children.

My Eight Children

Jamell—the oldest of the eight and my sister's first child. Cool is what I call him. All his friends call him Slim. He was twelve years old when my sister passed away. Cool lived with me since he was eight years old. I was trying to help my sister out and also give my boys an older-brother figure to look up to. He was a good student until my sister passed then his grades began to drop. His choice of friends were always the bad boys. He was a real warm and pleasant person with a big heart. He liked people and loved his family. My sister's death took a lot out of him as a person. He sort of shut down for a good long time. Losing his mother is a really big pill to swallow for sure. But for a son to lose his mother is a whole different kind of ball game. My nephew was truly lost without his mom. I continued to pray for his safety and well-being as a mother does, and it has kept him safe with minimal bumps and bruises. He is now thirty years old, not really able to work since he was shot in 2008, with two daughters, Serenity and Alana.

Latesia—the oldest girl of the eight and my sister's second child. Tesia is what I call her. She was eleven years old when my sister passed away. She struggled in school but was determined to graduate at any cost, and she did graduate. She was the little mama of the house. She helped me with cooking, cleaning, combing the girls' hair in the mornings for school, did the laundry, or whatever I needed her to help me with, and she never complained. She had a daughter named Caryssa in 2011 that passed away from complications. She took this really hard, but with the support and love of her family, she is doing much better. She comes from a family of strong women and that helps. She is now twenty-nine years old. She works in security and will be the one who will fill my shoes when the time comes. I know if I need her, she has my back. This is why I try to always have hers whenever I can.

Jeffrey—the second oldest boy of the eight and my first son. JP is what I call him.

He started off very angry about having to share his mother with his cousin. At the time, he really didn't understand the situation completely. Besides his anger, he kept his grades up. He was determined to become a successful person. He was not very sociable; he preferred to be alone. He visited his father, Jeff, as much as he could to get away from it all. He became very selfish about things that belonged to him. But one thing he did well was he knew how to save money and was slowly but surely becoming a junior loan shark like our granny at the age of ten. Family members would call my phone to talk to him for a loan with interest until they got paid because the entire family knew he kept money at all times. Jeffrey is currently employed in one of the city casinos. JP is now twenty-seven years old and has two daughters, Jayla and Ryan.

Tamisha—the second oldest girl of the eight and my sisters third child. She was seven years old when my sister passed away. Bookie is what I call her. She handled my sister's death the hardest of all the children. She became angry with everyone because she was too young to know how to handle the pain that she felt, having a great big empty space in her heart. The love of her mother is what she missed because Tonia showed her the most love of all maybe because she looked like her twin. She was confused and really did not understand why her mother was no longer around. She became an introvert, not very social, and struggled in school also. I saw happiness surface when she had her daughter, TaNiiya, for a very brief moment, then she was back to her unhappy, evil, and angry personality. She is currently a licensed CENA and appearing to be in a happy place in her life today, she is much nicer and friendlier to people.

Ramon—the third oldest boy of the eight and my second child. Yumpty is what I call him. He was my chocolate baby whom I had to protect from my granny because he was of a dark complexion. He was so jealous when the children came to live with us. He was only five years old and wanted his mother to himself. With Diamond being right behind him at three years old, it was loads of competition in the house for attention. Ramon was a very nice young man, well-mannered, and respectful.

He played sports throughout his whole childhood, with basketball becoming his number one love. He graduated and went on to college with a full-ride scholarship in basketball. Ramon is currently still in college studying to be an educator and is now twenty-four years old. He has no children.

Diamond—the third girl of the eight and my sister's fourth child. Fatty is what I call her. She was a very clingy child, too young to know there was a loss, and only saw me as mama 'cause this is what my boys called me, so she did also. Many people don't even know her natural mother passed away because she looks at me as her mother and I am. I couldn't move without Fatty right on my heels, whether it was to the eastern market or off early in the morning to buy the children something that they may have needed. Diamond watched me like a hawk. She knew I got up early, so she would get up and go with me for half of the day. She was great in school from the time she started. She played basketball and studied drama she was the best cheerleader ever. Diamond strived to be noticed just like I did as a child. She was very friendly, polite, and kind. All the teachers loved her. She had loads of friends. Diamond is currently in college studying to be an RN, is now twenty-two years old, and she has no children.

Whitney—the fourth girl of the eight and my sister's fifth child. Baby Girl is what I call her. She was twenty-three months when my sister passed. She had been in the hospital from the time she was born until she was nine months, which is when I picked her up from the hospital. I even had to name her cause she was still named Baby Girl Franklin. Once Tonia was better, Whitney went home with her for close to a year before Tonia became extremely ill and could not take care of her anymore. Whitney came home with a heart monitor and needed breathing machines from time to time due to her prenatal birth. Baby Girl was born when Tonia was only five months pregnant but survived against all the doctors' diagnoses. Whitney was a miracle baby. No one could touch her or look at her for too long; she would cry. The only person that she went to was Tesia.

The doctors said she suffered from a form of disconnection disorder from the loss of her mother. She struggled in school from day one from a learning disability that made it really hard for her to learn. Whitney played basketball until she found out her face may be hit and quit the team after a few games. She is currently in school to get her GED, also becoming a Detroit Builder. I'm proud she didn't give up. She is now twenty years old and has no children.

Terrick—the fourth boy of the eight and my third son. Doo Doo Whop is what I call him. He has always been a very loving and friendly person from birth, the easygoing one. He was an average student in school. He suffered from a slight learning disability also, which we later discovered was the blame of his and Whitney's first—and second-grade teacher that they shared. They were found to be incompetent when they got to middle school and were still struggling. Terrick liked getting a lot of attention. He danced and sang in school concerts, had plenty of friends, and was happy with such a big family especially because he was the baby boy. He played basketball until he graduated and enrolled into Marygrove College with a scholarship where he continued to play on the team. Terrick is now nineteen years old, currently a sophomore, and has no children.

As you see, I have eight children. I felt privileged to have a man take care of me and also my sister's five children. I was willing to go the limit for him and with him, and I definitely ended up doing just that. Do you think men are going to be lined up trying to get with me for anything more than sex? This was my thinking pattern at the time. It was no holds barred for Mr. Colbert, and I can honestly say I put in more energy with him than any other man in my life.

Was it a job being the woman of a drug dealer? I had to deal with all the neighborhood freaks and tramps that would fuck anyone with a few dollars or the crackheads that were willing to suck dick or get fucked in the ass for a piece of crack it was terrible. Not only that, his body was looking so good when he came home. He weighed 185 lbs. and was 5'11".

He could dress his ass off, and always smelled so good. He was very confident, a mild mannered person that had a smile to die for, and was easy to like, plus he knew just about everyone in the city so I always felt protected.

Mook just blew me off my feet our first two years after we were married in Las Vegas on 7/11/00—his lucky number 711. He was a gambler since he was a kid and pretty lucky on the crap table. I stood at the table all night mesmerized by him when he is on his lucky spree. He talks plenty of shit and keeps those dice hitting and the drinks coming. He would watch my every move, and I knew this. He made me feel wanted, sexy, and loved all the things most women want. The ingredient is very simple, but men don't take the time to just pay attention to how a woman responds to these free and simple things. Instead they think it's about a big dick, a hard fuck, and money. I can't say they are not important but not the most important. Whenever Mook watched me dance, he would rub his hands together real slow and put on this big Chester the cheese cat smile. My family would say he looked at me like I was steak and potatoes. All I know is I loved every moment of it.

We partied, traveled, purchased drugs, sold drugs, then he started using drugs again. Before long he was back in jail for ninety days, one year here, two and a half years there, and so on. Mook's drug habit got so bad the he stole my entire state income tax check from our joint account and lied by telling me he was gambling at the casino whenever I would question him about our bank statement. He was so hooked on drugs this time that he would drive from the hood to downtown just to withdraw the money from the ATM in the casino so he could tell me he had a problem with gambling, but he really had a terrible addiction to heroin. A drug he had never used before to my knowledge. But I could be wrong about that too. This was the beginning of the end for us.

I began having problems with a hood rat bitch over this nigga because he was using her house to sell his shit from and they started fuckin' around when they got high off the dope together. I knew all about it, but I let it ride for a good while before I had to go to the hoe house and drop some Ds on her ass. She disrespected me in the worst way. She wanted me to know she was with him by opening her mouth and being heard. Rule number 1 for you chicks that are fuckin' around with a woman's husband, remain anonymous, keep your mouth shut, stay indoors with him, and don't be dumb enough to try and get pregnant if you know what's best for you.

A scorned wife is nothing to play with. I ended up in jail after fighting this girl with five children all by different fathers, and she pressed charges to the fullest. I stayed in jail for a week before Mook had to pay her off and talked her into dropping the charges. I promised that day that I would never love a man again that much to have me end up in jail over him. My lack of trust level was dangerously high. Mook could not go to the bathroom without being accused of something or someone.

I never was a jealous woman with anyone I ever dated. But I was not going to be disrespected by no one man or woman. Our relationship was suffering, and I really tried to get things back the way they were, but when your heart has been broken, it takes a whole lot for it to heal.

Mook went to jail for the last time before we separated in 2005 for drunk driving. This was now his third offense, and a DUI was very serious. They gave him eighteen months. This was eighteen months too long for me. I only waited nine months before I woke up one day and decided that I should not have to keep going through this shit like I am in prison. This motherfucker would not be waiting for me to get out of jail all these times. It's been a total of close to three years that I had waited before.

It was December 3. I had an ay birthday party celebrating my thirty-ninth birthday. I met this guy named Lou through a friend. He could not talk this night; he had laryngitis.

Since I was very tipsy off the drinks, I played around with him most of the night. It was a blast to be enjoying myself after all this time. I was *free.*

Just a Sex Thang

I was somewhat intrigued by Lou. He was totally different from the type of guy I am usually attracted to. He was sort of on the chubby side. He wore prescription glasses and was a nerd to some degree, and I could tell that he wanted to be a thug all his life, but it just wasn't in him. He let me take charge over him right off the rip. I was taking his money out of his hands. I was telling him to shut the fuck up, and he did. I took his hat, coat, and scarf off him at my party and walked around the club all drunk and carrying on. Just simply fucking with him all night long. He thought it was cute. He kept smiling and shit. That's when I knew I was somewhat like a dominatrix without the physical abuse. He was completely turned on by all this disrespect and so was I.

Lou wanted me so bad that night, I could see it in his eyes. He had never met a chick like "Tish" before in his life. She was so straightforward, said whatever was on her mind, most of all she brought out the real freak in him. From the looks of it, we both needed some release. I invited him my after party at my house. He never showed up because he knew that the area where I lived, the state troopers had taken over because the local police were all fired or laid off because of the recession the city was broke and could not afford to pay them. It was a heavy snowstorm by the time we made it home, and I went straight to sleep anyway. We talked on the phone the next day and he explained to me that he could afford to be bothered by the state boys because he had been drinking to would jump behind the wheel no matter what. He told me that he felt intimidated by me and that I was too overly aggressive.

Actually this was his biggest interest in me. I just played it off as if I didn't know this. We didn't have sex the first day, but it wasn't long before we did. It was less than a week, something I have never done before. Even with the doctor I waited over a year.

The main reason I sleep with him so soon was because I was suffering from a flaming hot pussy! I had not had sex for over nine months, and I needed some dick bad. I just wanted to come hard and long. We talked every day all day long from the day of my party. Until finally I said, "Lou, do you want to fuck me?" He laughed and responded, "What are you talking about, girl?" I repeated the question, "Do you want to fuck me?" Quickly he said, "When?" I said, "Today, right now." He was like, "You're tripping me out. I said, "Why? Because I asked what you wanted to ask since we met."

He said, "Now you acting like a nigga." I told him, "I can show you I'm not a nigga." "Where?" he said. I said, "Where can you afford to take me 'cause it won't be here at my house." He paused for a moment and then said, "Give me a minute. I will have to call you back." He had mentioned over the past few days that he cared for his parents because they were older. This was why he still lived at home at the age of thirty-eight. Not long after, he called me back to say, "Are you going to meet me, or are we riding together?" I told him I was going to follow him but asked where to. "The Troy Hotel," he said. "I will meet you at the liquor store by my house in thirty minutes." We had not seen each other in almost a week and clearly didn't know who each other was when we got to the store. I just felt like doing something out of character.

He said, "Damn, I thought you had really big titties." I smiled and said, "Nope, you got me mixed up with someone else, but I do have some nice pretty titties with some suckable nipples on them." I opened my shirt to expose myself, and he could see what I was talking about through the blouse I was wearing and agreed. Then he said, "But I did remember you were rocking a ball fade with waves." I said, "Oh yeah, you like it?" He said, "Hell yeah, I like it." We walked to the counter, ordered some Hennessy, then I stepped aside for him to make the purchase. He stepped behind me and whispered, "Girl, you don't know what you're getting yourself into." I answered, "Oh yes, I do," and walked out to my car.

I followed him to the Troy Hotel. Before getting out of the car, I called my best friend to tell her where I was and with whom. We got out of our cars, walked into the hotel, then it struck me. "Did you buy some condoms?" Lou looked at me like I was speaking in tongues. "What, girl, why didn't you say something when we were at the store?"

"So you get down like that with this shit out here?" He said, "No! But now I have to find a store out here. I will ride with you." It took a minute, but we found a CVS, and he took care of this little problem then back to the hotel we went.

I had a sexy piece of lingerie; it was ice blue, very cute, and he enjoyed it very much. We drank all the Hennessy and smoked some trees. I was feeling so relaxed with him. We laughed and talked about all kinds of things. He was very intelligent. He kept up on what was going on in the world. I could tell he was no dummy. It was obvious that he read the newspaper daily. Very interesting, I thought this may become more than just my first fling. He asked if I was hungry. I was, but who wants to have sex on a full stomach? So I said we can eat later.

He reached over and kissed me very soft and sweet. He made a sound like huh and stared at me. I asked, "Is there a problem?" He said, "Not at all, not at all." It was on and popping. He rubbed my body down from head to toe. I needed this more than he would ever know. I was tense as fuck. Once he relaxed my entire body, he went straight for the gusto. He spread my legs open and laid his face on my pussy and took a deep breath, smelling my hot juices. He looked at me as he pulled my panties down very slow. His tongue was hot and wet. I wanted to feel his lips sucking my clit ever so softly. I closed my eyes while he sucked and sucked my pussy until I creamed in his mouth like a scoop of ice cream from the Mr. Softy Ice Cream truck.

Lou said, "So it's been a minute for you I see". I said," it's been months 9 to be exact". Lou pulled his body up over me. His dick was rock hard. I slid down his boxers to apply the condom but I stopped him, I took him inside my mouth.

I wanted to give him the same pleasure he had just given me, so I sucked it slow, deep and gentle. My mouth was dripping wet with passion. I was horny as a hostage, aiming to suck his brains out. He was loving it. "Yeah, baby, suck it," Lou moaned. I continued sucking too.

Pulling it out to see his reaction, he was on top of the world, and I liked making him feel like that. I felt powerful and in control. So now I have to let him know what he was in for, I stroked his shaft and sucked some more until, I popped it off like a real bitch does and let it pour out the side of my mouth very slowly down my neck, my breast, over my nipples, down my stomach to fill my navel, down to my pussy as I laid down to begin rubbing my clit and fingering myself in a vigorous motion until I came again. Lou just said, "Girl, you're something else." I said, "I know right."

I'm not going to be fake; I was feeling him too. Even though he was a big boy he knew how to please me better than a lot of the men I had been with in the past. Lou was very light on me and his feet.

I didn't know if it was because I was lonely, horney or did I really like him for him. It took me some time to sort my feelings out. I was tired of Mook, I knew, but was I ready to leave him for good? I did not know. The one thing that I did know was that Lou and I had great sex together. He allowed me to have my way with him. If I wanted to be held, he held me. If I wanted to be massaged, he massaged me. If I wanted my pussy sucked, he sucked it. Never any complaints, just all pleasure, and I did the same for him. We were not in a relationship, so this made it easy. No strings attached, plus I was still married to Mook.

He had a preplanned trip to California to visit family for Christmas, so this meant I would not see him for two weeks, but before he left, I gave him something to remember me by. I sucked his dick for twenty minutes in my dining room with my father in the living room. He was so hard, it took everything in him not to scream. When he finally relieved himself in my mouth, he held me so tight. He had tears in his eyes.

He called me daily for the duration of his road trip. It took twenty-four hours to get there from Michigan.

He talked to me almost the entire way there. He called at least five times a day while he was in California and the whole way back. Once he got back in the city, he came straight to mama. We both could not wait. When he pulled up to the house, I ran out to the minivan and gave him the business in the back area of the van. The windows were fogged. It was snowing heavily. The van was covered. We both exploded at the same time. Our days from then on, we were together. We both needed each other's company. Our conversations were always interesting. We liked to talk to one another about anything and everything.

Lou was in love with me, and it showed. He didn't have much money, but what he had he spent. He was recently laid off from the plant American Axle and was only receiving unemployment checks. He spent all his free time with me. He cooked for me and the children, he kept my house clean, and he even did the laundry. We shared most of my wildest fantasies together. We would fuck any and everywhere. One time we went out for a ride and decided to stop at the park to smoke a blunt. Once we were done, we got out of the car to take a walk, when I noticed a bike trail. I gave him the look that I do when it's on and popping (that means when I am ready to get fucked).

I took his hand and led him to a tree not far from the trail entrance. I knew we would be seen. I pulled down my shorts and panties, grabbed hold of a tree, bent over to show Lou my booty, and he got hard instantly. Lou put his dick in then began to enter very slowly I assume the weed helped a lot but it was great. He got so far up inside of my ass, we were both frozen and in the moment of ecstasy. I had only experienced anal sex with Mook once before this.

I had heard how good of a feeling it was supposed to be from all my friends and a few family members. But my one experience with Mook was terrible. So I never tried it again I guess Mook was so eager I let him try it, he was just too rough.

But Lou had my ass dripping wet as an ocean, and before long, four teenage boys came riding through on their bikes to witness the two of us in the midst of our climax.

His hot lava began to leak from within and down my leg. He had come so much, we were stuck together for a moment.

Sex was everywhere from that point on with Lou. No more fucking we began making love. In my truck, during a concert downtown in the middle of a thunderstorm while everyone was running to their cars, we cracked the window so we could be heard. It was so intense that whenever someone got close to the truck, they would stop in their tracks in the rain to listen and see where the sex noises were coming from. The windows were so fogged, they could not see inside the car.

The smell of good sex is the greatest fragrance to me, but there is a different fragrance with every partner and one that a women can remember. We had sex so much that my father felt that all he was doing for me was fucking me and feeding me. And Daddy was right about that, but this was all I needed at the time. Because I am one of those women who have multiple orgasms, he was good at taking care of all of them, no matter how many of them there were. Not many men could handle the job, so he just filled the position for three whole years. I knew from our first conversation he was a dreamer, but that was fine at the time because I wasn't looking for a commitment.

Until, I got tired of his lies he had a baby before we met by a married woman so he was beginning to have baby mama drama. Something I had no time for. I love children as you know. But I didn't have time to be dealing with that mess. So we ended our relationship in September of 2008. I got back with Mook for a few months nothing had changed with him so we divorced then my sons and I got a penthouse apartment and shared some time together for a change.

It was nice living with my sons for the first time only the four of us since they were kids. My daddy passed away and my body began shutting down.

My Lupus flared up so bad that I dropped weight from a size 12 to a size 4. I thought I was about to die for the first time since being diagnosed with the disease. The stress of his death will not take me out I was determined of this so. I had to take a medical leave from work that started off as short term disability but ended up becoming long term for many years. I could not afford living in the apartment any longer so I moved into my grandmother's house to help me save money for a year.

True Love Returns

It was January 20, 2009. We had the first black president in my lifetime. I can't believe it, but yes, it's true. I actually lived to see this, and I'm proud to say I did. Today was his inauguration. What else could happen today that I would have never imagined? None other than a blast from so far in my past that it fucked me up. One of my childhood friends had become seriously ill. This brought a lot of us back together, and it was nice to get back in touch with my true childhood friends. From the first time we hooked back up, we thought about each other every moment of the day. Leon Blankenship, the one who took my virginity, had shown back up on the scene. Exactly thirty years from when we met for the very first time when I was eleven years old. Looking good as hell! Smelling like a real man should, neat as fuck from head to toe as he always was. Damn, Leon!

We began dating every night we talked about the past and how things would have been if we had stayed together all those years. We laughed and really enjoyed spending time together again.

Then Leon said something that shocked me death. He said "Do you know if you would have had our baby it would have been about to turn thirty years old? My mouth dropped then I said, "What are you talking about Leon"?

He said, Remember you called me and told me that you missed your period when your family moved with your granny. Then you called me after you got out of the hospital and said that you had a miscarriage and that you were almost three months pregnant so that was my baby.

We had sex in November around Thanksgiving and you had the miscarriage in February add it up Lesia that was our baby.

I couldn't believe that he remembered the dates and months that this all happen. But he was right. For close to thirty years I thought I had that miscarriage by Mook. But it was my first LEON.

This is why I loved you so much for all these years you were my first and you are going to be my last.

Every time I tried to get with you I heard that you were married again so I'm not letting you get away this time. I have known you every move, who you were with and if you were happy or not.

Mr. Blankenship must love me and the baby had to be important for him to bring it up now. I truly don't remember calling him at all. I didn't want anyone to know my Secret but this goes to show you that we were young as hell when this happen between us. But true love has no age limit on it.

No one knew but the two of us I guess because it wasn't about anybody else but us.

Leon had been in prison for several years and planned on finding me once he came home is what he claimed to have told a few people that we knew. He kept his promise to himself. He came home in search of finding the one who had his back from the start. At the time, he was too young and naive to understand this—that Lesia was the best girl for him. Instead he had to bump his head not once or twice but three times, then ended up in prison. Come to think about it, this was what had to happen, or else he never would have taken time to evaluate his life and come to the conclusion of locating me.

We dated for less than one month before he proposed in front of my family and friends on Super Bowl Sunday. It brought tears to my eyes. This was the first time out of my other marriages that I was proposed to in the proper manner. I must admit it was a mind-blowing experience for me. I wasn't quite sure if I was really ready to go right back into the whole marriage thing although I loved being married and being a wife.

As you know, I have tried this a few times already without success of a lifetime commitment. I hesitated for a good while until he asked for a second time. I turned around because I was in the middle of washing dishes to say, "Are you for real?"

Leon replied, "Yes. I asked your brother for permission to have your hand in marriage since your father is deceased. He is the next male figure in your life to ask, so I did." My brother gave his approval with a nod of his head, then I said yes. Everyone was clapping and smiling. I was still in shock, I think, for a while. Leon told me to start planning the wedding right away. We were married that following August 8, 2009. It was my first traditional church wedding.

Another first with Leon. Our wedding was beautiful. I chose the eighth of August to honor my sister whose birthday was on the seventh.

We got married in church because it was something I never did, and maybe this is why the other marriages didn't last. I believe it's because we didn't do it in the house of the Lord. I said yes because Leon is the one my mother always liked right from the very start. Last but not least, he reminded me of my daddy, very straightforward and not taking no for an answer.

During the reception, a small brawl broke out between the younger adults, which we later found out at the end of the reception. That this was only a distraction to allow some asshole to hit our wishing well. Yes, I said it. Someone took all our cards, gift cards, and money that were given to us on our special day. Our wedding day! Really? Since this happened, Leon and I didn't have the funds to pay our DJ, photographer, or go on our one week Hawaiian honeymoon that we planned to leave for the following evening. We were so hurt because of this that after the reception, we both went home and just laid on the bed in dismay about the entire incident. Sex was the last thing on our minds, so the marriage was not even consummated that night. I slept in my wedding gown and Leon in his tuxedo. We woke up the next morning laughing about it. We were in real true love all over again.

We closed the deal on our first home four days after the wedding, with the assistance of Leon's mother, Mildred, my mother-in-law. It's a two-family-unit brick home with five bedrooms, a fireplace, full basement, 2 bathrooms, kitchens, living rooms and dining rooms, with a very nice and large deck built onto the house in the backyard that accommodates at least thirty people for our outdoor events. We both love bringing family and friends together for a good ole time. Leon and I have so many things in common, like having cookouts, dancing, living life to the fullest, and working hard to make life as easy as possible.

Now I'm Mrs. Leon Blankenship, just when I told myself I would never get married ever again. So my new motto is Never Say Never. I think I finally got it right, a man who would not allow me to run over him, works his ass off, will not beat my ass, but keep me in my place as a woman. For a change, I can just be that—a woman. This is what I wanted all along, to be in a position that I could really relate to, not just taking care of people and always trying to handle it all, not being able to show my true female emotions. All I have to do is just be me. It is taking a lot out of me going through this transformation at such a late age. I am now forty-two. Leon has to deal with a lot of stress because I am always challenging him about everything. I do not know how to be the second in charge in my household, so we have a rough road ahead to conquer and we will.

With our children being all adults, they are not as close as we both wish they were, but we are working on having more family functions that will include only our children and Leon and I to hopefully bring us all closer. Leon and his children's mom don't have the best relationship, to be honest. But we can all be in the room together and get along. I have a great relationship with my children's father. I am so blessed to have a great relationship also with his wife. This is the way it should be with all families just because the marriage or relationship ends, we're still all connected in many ways, so be adults and make it work for yourself and for the children.

Being married to Leon has been an adventure. With him being the only child, he expects everything to revolve around him.

With me being a woman who has had a man that provided everything for me, it's a hard and bumpy ride for us. Learning to compromise is something we know nothing about. Leon is more about material things, like cars, clothes, jewelry, and his appearance, and I, on the other hand, am more concerned with improving our household, stocks and bonds, retirement savings, and vacationing. Appearance is important but last on my list, and I will sacrifice on things that I want for what I need. Opposites attract, I guess, because this keeps us communicating about something every day, whether it's an argument or agreement.

This is what marriage is all about—working together to make it work and never giving up on it if you can. We truly love one another. It's not easy; we have to do our work if we want it. It's our second anniversary. Leon has been saving every dime he has been making from either doing a roof or cutting grass or painting. He is always busy doing something to make a dollar. My main thing that I love about him is that he will make it happen one way or another. How all men should be? I have to thank Granddaddy Bob for this one. He was Leon's stepfather who taught him to lay roofs when he was only thirteen years old, a free trade that he was lucky to have learned. We received bad news of his grandmother passing away; she lived in Alabama. We made plans to travel by car to attend the funeral.

I have never gone to the south in my entire life although it was something I always wanted to experience. Now it was happening. My visions of the south were all bad. I pictured his family living off dirt roads with their homes sitting on the ground, no basements, or grass along with an old hound dog lying on the front porch. The *Beverly Hillbillies* show must have made a big impact on me as a kid. Boy was I wrong! I mean way wrong at that. When we pulled up to the land, I was shocked. It was beautiful to see black people own such a large amount of land. I asked how much land is was and was told she owned over forty acres. And his entire generation lived on his grandmother's land. This was a wonderful sight to see. At that moment, I felt very proud to be a Blankenship.

There was Lauderdale Lane, Blankenship Boulevard, and McMillon Road, just to name a few of the streets named after the families. I slept better than I ever have while we were there. I believe it was the peacefulness that reminded me of when I was a child. Hearing the sounds of crickets gives me a certain comfort. The sounds relaxed me in a way that I had not felt in decades. I loved it. Even though I didn't go out as much as I would have liked, I did get the best rest that I have had in a long time. I look forward to returning to Alabama sometime soon.

Upon our arrival back in Detroit, we didn't have time to even unpack before more bad news hit us. Leon's parole officer had been to the house while we were away, and Leon had a warrant for his arrest for leaving out of state without permission. In fact, Leon did go to the office to request the right to leave, but his officer was out of the office on vacation and the person who was her relief had Leon wait until she saw her people before she was going to see him.

His instincts told him she was going to refuse his request, so he went anyway in hopes of not being found out.

We decided to stay away the one extra day in Alabama was when she dropped by because she was aware that Leon had come to the office without an appointment and heard he left without being seen by another PO. The very next day, his PO was at our home with two other officers to pick up Leon and with a search warrant for the house. They were all in our bedroom drawers and closets looking for anything to pin on my husband.

Then boom! She found the pound of marijuana that I purchased to help with my body pains caused by my lupus. I hurried to locate my paperwork regarding all my elements. She was shocked. She looked at me and said, "What don't you have?" I stood there with a look of uncertainty, then she said, "I still have to take it from here. Drugs can't be in the home of a felon."

The good thing is she didn't charge Leon with the weed, but she also never reported taking the weed from the house either. Leon had to do ninety days in a camp for this action which could have been much worse.

Once he completed this, he had no more run-ins with the police for anything.

Now off parole, my man has to get his life on track, take care of his child support issues, clean up his credit, establish some credit, get his license—he even got his chauffeur's license and, most of all, a *job*! It all fell right into place within a year of being home. He had accomplished each and every one of these things. There's no limit to what a man can do as long as he believes in himself and has a strong minded woman to stand beside him on his journey. We are a proven fact of this. We're now off and running into our future together and making big moves is our goal. We laugh, cry, argue, fuss, and fight, but we are determined to make it last forever.

Just when I thought I had the man of my dreams and feeling happy again, my health took a turn. I'm not sure if it was because the winter was approaching fast, something I hated to see coming caused my stress level to rise or what, but my daughter took me to my regular doctor's appointment. I felt fine all morning with no idea my blood pressure was through the roof. The nurse took my pressure then ran out of the room in a dash to return telling me I was about to be taken to the ER. I asked why. She said, "You're threatening a stroke. Your pressure is 210 over 190." I began to panic as they wheeled me there and rush me onto a gurney.

Before long, doctors were coming and going, constantly asking me if I had a headache. But I didn't feel any pain whatsoever. After being there for a few hours, they told me I was being admitted right away. I lost the feeling of my left side from my shoulder to just above my knee. The medication that was placed in my IV began to work. I was out for I don't know how long before I was awakened by the voices of several ladies. I opened my eyes to see 4747. I screamed where I am because no one was around that I recognized.

A nurse came to my side and said to me, "You're in a special ward to be monitored. Why are you so afraid?" I told her, "I have to get out of this room or else I'm going to die."

She said everything she thought would calm me down but nothing worked. Shortly after, a doctor walked in and stood next to my bed with a very serious look on his face. He asked, "Can you lift your leg?" I tried, but I couldn't, so he took an instrument out of his pocket and rubbed down my foot and asked if I felt it. I said no, I didn't.

He walked to the top of the bed above my head so I could not see him and said, "Lift your left arm." I couldn't. Then he said, "Lift your right arm." I did without any delay. "Lift your right leg." I did also without delay. He walked out of the room without saying another word. Now the nurse was back to my bedside, asking why I said I was going to die if I stayed in the room. I responded because of the number 4747. "What does that mean to you?" I said, "It's the age my mother was when she died—forty-seven, not a lucky number."

She wrote it down and said she will be back soon. I looked around the room and noticed there was a Jacuzzi tub in the corner and thought what hospital am I in and what I did to get in this room 'cause I had no health insurance at the time. It was so nice, I couldn't believe it. So the next person that I saw I had to ask who was paying for all of it. There must be a mix up somewhere. When the nurse entered the room, I said, "Nurse, who's paying for this room? I don't have health insurance." She told me not to worry about that, "The head doctor had you placed here."

I was in the hospital for over a month going through all kinds of tests to figure out why this happened to me. Stroke was ruled out. There were no signs of it on my CAT scan or MRI. After being in the hospital for about one week, they determined my central nervous system had shut down on me. I was taken to the rehabilitation department so I could begin the steps of walking again. It was interesting and scary all at the same time. Just like that, I went from standing, running, and walking on my own to being helped up and helped down.

It was amazing how my brain was running the show all by itself. Those three pounds are so much more powerful than we can ever imagine.

This nervous shut down also affected my memory like simple things I used to know without a second guess. I went to therapy daily, sometimes more than once a day. It wasn't long before I was up and taking steps on my own. I shed a lot of tears going through the process. It was so emotional for me. It reminded me of when my mother was hit by the car and I cared for her, watching her go from a full body cast to taking her to therapy so she could learn to walk again.

I was discharged on November 10, going home with instructions for daily exercise bathing, walking, and transportation tips. Leon was fully responsible for taking care of me, which lasted only two weeks before he just snapped on me. He couldn't take it, seeing me as an indolent, so he started pushing me harder and harder by the day. "Get out of the tub on your own. Pull up, you can do it." He would walk away and wait in the hallway. This made me angry, but I did it on my own. I was walking with assistance for a few months. I have permanent left-side hemiparesis for the rest of my life. My legs give out on me if I allow my stress level to rise to a high degree. So I now try my best to avoid all things that cause me stress, meaning dealing with Leon also.

I received a call from my sister/friend Lori asking me if I had to have a procedure done that was very critical, what hospital would I trust. I of course told her the hospital I was recently discharged from. They treated me well and also took excellent care of me. I asked, "What's going on, Lori?" She told me, "Don't worry about it. I just wanted to know your opinion." She called me again to say she was having surgery in a few days and would stop by with her daughter. I invited them to dinner. Leon prepared his famous burgers and fries. We sat at the dinner table laughing and talking while we enjoyed our meal.

Lori made Leon and I promise we would bring her Thanksgiving dinner up to the hospital after the surgery. We agreed. The morning of the surgery, told me she had to be there by 5 am I planned to call her that morning to pray with her but I overslept, so I didn't get to talk to her before she went in. I didn't have any bad feelings about the surgery at all. I knew my sister/ friend was covered by the blood of Jesus. Lori was a god fearing woman all of her life. So I had absolutely no worries all early morning, but I began to worry once I called her children and they didn't know anything many hours after she should have been in recovery. Every hour on the hour I called her sons back for a follow-up. Later that day, my godson, her oldest son, called me to say she was in a coma. The surgery didn't go well; they ran into some problems.

Things were not looking good. I went against doctors' orders and went to the hospital with her children for support. Walking in the room just broke my heart. To see my friend this way was heart-wrenching. I never in a million years imagined I would be there looking at her in that state. Lori was never sick as we grew up. She was always the visitor, not the patient. I tried to stay strong for the children, but only God knows I wanted to pass out. As I sat next to her in the critical care unit, I reflected back on our lives together, all the good times we shared along with the bad. All in all, we loved each other no matter what.

Lori passed away. I couldn't stop crying my heart was torn apart not again. This was my first time losing a close friend. I starting getting sick from the day of her passing. My immune system was running wild. Leon took me to the ER I was diagnosed with pneumonia on my birthday which was the day of her viewing, I went straight to the funeral home after I left the hospital. I had to see my friend for the last time even if it meant I was making myself worse. I was unable to attend the funeral. All act of God, he knew I couldn't handle it so he set me down once more.

Now dealing with the loss of my two sisters, my mother and father, plus dealing with all my illnesses above other things, I promised them all that I will never give and continue to fight to be here for all the children as best I can. I will never forget them.

At times I feel alone even with all my children, grandchildren, friends, family, and a husband who I know dearly loves me. You just need certain people there at certain times that used to make things seem much easier. But life goes on, and we have to continue to live.

Through the good, bad, and the ugly. If it was all roses 100 percent of the time, we would forget about our number 1 and only true friend *Jesus*.

A friend of Leon's found out about a program that helps ex-cons that was funded by the city of Detroit. It was an eight-week class that taught him about agriculture. Once he completed the program, he graduated and moved on to work for the company for a season before he began working for a major construction company that he is currently still employed with. He loves working. He says it makes him feel like a real man, being able to bring a check home to his wife to pay the bills and to see me without any stress as I was when we first got back together. Leon is a good man. I just had to tighten up a few areas where he was not polished. I'm managing this task still to date, and I enjoy watching him bloom like a flower daily. It makes me happy.

To witness his strengths in all ways, he has become a better son, father, man, and husband because we believed in one another's love. I have warned my daughters not to date or even think about marrying a man that's an only child unless their ready to do a whole lot of work. I sit back whenever I'm alone at the house and think about my life. Would I have done anything different? Hell new! All the things that I went through was God's plan for me to become the person I am today—a 100 percent woman who's willing to do whatever it takes.

A hardworking woman, at home, work, or play, I get it done. Running my household, taking care of my man alone with doing what makes Elisa happy is what my life has turned out to be, and I love it.

I could not run from who I am—Arlesia Marie Franklin-Blankenship, daughter of one hell of a woman, Mrs. Sandra Gail Franklin.

Tighten Up Loose Ends

After my mama and sister passed away, Daddy lived with me, almost everywhere I lived. He began using drugs shortly after my sister died. The loss of her took a big toll on him. During our talks, he told me that he hoped one day he and Mama would have rekindled their marriage and that he never thought in a million years that she would have died before him. He also told me that he never stopped loving her. I asked him, "Do you regret how you treated her when you had her?" He said, "Yes, more than anyone will ever know." Daddy ended up passing away from an enlarged heart and kidney failure in 2008. I will never forget him. He taught me to cook all the major holiday meals with love, and every Thanksgiving I think of him most.

Daddy's Girl

My granny and I began to build a great relationship in 1995 after I finally asked her one day why she hated me so much as a child. She replied, "I never hated you. Why would you say something like that?" I said, "Because you never called me by my name. It was always 'Your black ass this or that,' you made me feel like you didn't like me all the time." Granny had a surprised look on her face as in disbelief. Then she said, "I never knew I made you feel that way. It must have been the liquor that made me that way toward you. When I used to drink alcohol, I would become a very mean person." Then she said, "I'm so sorry I made you feel like that." I forgave her, then from that day, we began to talk regularly. Much to my surprise, I found that Granny and I had so many things in common. But most of all, I learned that you can't judge a person from the outside. People have many layers; some people need to peel down a few layers before you find the real person.

I wrote a poem in her obituary that some didn't feel was appropriate to do, but it was the truth about our relationship, and I basically was thanking her for making me a stronger person because my battles with my own granny as a child made me a better woman.

Our relationship came late but. right on time.

Thank you for being honest and apologizing

Love, your second oldest granddaughter.

Courtnay and I are still best friends. I have given her the title of my longest and dearest friend. No one can ever replace her. She was a bridesmaid at my wedding to Leon, and we talk much more and keep one another abreast of what's going on in our lives. She is the mother of a teenage son, is very involved in her church, and makes her own jewelry. Court is dating a very nice gentleman that I had the pleasure of meeting at my forty-seventh birthday dinner. She appears happier than I have ever seen her, and I hope to be a part of her wedding soon.

Thanks for being my friend for thirty-three years (Stank).

Tony and I talk or see each other almost other day. He is now the father of ten children and happily married to his wife, Dorrinda. He is still cutting hair and is the proud grandfather of eight. He is very involved in his church and is also a member of God Fathers

Only, an organization aimed toward helping our young black men who need a male role model in their lives.

He has finally settled down and learned to sit still and be committed to a relationship.

We began adulthood lifestyles very early, bro, and we have been blessed to be alive today after all we have been through.

I am so happy that we have been able to share some of our older years together. Lastly, you are the complete replica of our daddy the older you get as I am of our mama.

Remember what mama always told us, all we have is each other.

It's only you and I left, little brother. Let's make it count.

Peaches and I talk all the time. We're both looking forward to our big move to Florida to avoid all the snow and cold weather. Peaches has been diagnosed with fibromyalgia, which causes her to deal with much more pain than I do with my lupus, but they are both very painful illnesses. She is married and has three children and a few grandchildren. We have great conversations and always support each other emotionally.

Peach, it's been great knowing that you are around at the times when I need to talk to my mama. You fill in for her so well.

Jeff and I have the relationship that all parents should have. We don't talk often, but when we do, it's always pleasant. He is married, with three daughters I all adore. He has been the best father any child could imagine. He has two granddaughters and still works hard for a company that he has been employed with for over thirty years.

A prime example of a good man, husband, and father, he has taught our son, JP, to be a good father and to be a hard worker just like he has been.

We met really young, and I learned a lot from being in your company. The one thing I love most about you is that you never changed who you are.

Thank you for being a great father and friend.

Terrick and I have a wonderful relationship also. He has dedicated his entire life to our sons and his daughter by his ex-wife. He kept them busy with every activity possible to try and keep them off the streets. He also kept them in church every Sunday. Both of our sons graduated high school, one with a full scholarship and the other with a partial scholarship. They have traveled all over the US with AAU basketball teams. Both were ambassadors of the United States. He currently works for a major mattress company along with being the proud owner of his own delivery company that our sons help him operate.

Thanks for being the *best father ever.*

You are one of a kind, and I hope you never change.

Mook and I talk from time to time just to check on one another's health and well-being. Mook is currently suffering from a hip problem that caused him to walk with a dragging limp on his right side. He has not had any more children. He is in a relationship with another woman with a lot of children. I guess he just loves being around kids or just the whole family feeling.

I will always have a special love for Mook because of his strength and support for me when I needed him most. My mother and sister were gone, and I really had no one there for me at that time in my life but him.

Mook has always been a good genuine person who will definitely be walking through the golden gates of heaven with no doubt in my mind because, first and foremost, he has always loved God, his mother, father, his wife, his children, his friends, and anyone who crossed his path.

God knew when to bring you back in my life and also when to remove you from it.

You will always mean the world to me and the kids.

Lou and I don't talk at all anymore. My last recollection of him was that he has a few children, never got married, still living at home with his mom, partying, and hanging in the streets daily.

Lying constantly. Still not taking life seriously. And brings me up whenever he comes in the company of anyone I know. But I want to thank him for being in life at a time that I needed all those things. Not taking life seriously, living for the moment with no holds barred. It was fun while it lasted, but it never could have been more than what it was. A time passer is what he was, and I am so glad that's all he was. Now as a full grown woman, I could not have done anything with him but played. Since I look at life so much more serious than that, I am so happy it was what it was.

I hope all is well for you and one day you grow up.

Leon and I are still married. We have a new puppy named Roco. Six granddaughters, one grandson and one on the way. We're looking forward to relocating to Florida for the winter months. Due to my illness, being in a warmer climate will be better for me then returning home during the summer. In the meantime, he will work with his company while I continue working on my next books. We have decided to dedicate ourselves to this marriage and do the work to keep it together.

Arlesia, Lesia Lipz & Tish are all still together trying to understand each other. It's amazing that when I look over my life trying to make since of why I made certain choices or why I didn't do certain things. I discovered after evaluating myself that the reason I married so many times was because I loved being a wife to my man. But the main reason was I believed it made me appear to be a better woman than my mama was.

I unconsciously blamed my mama for my daddy leaving the home. At the time I had no idea that he was beating on her often. I spend many years comparing our lives and was blown away once I finally began discovering how many of the same path we had taken in our life. When I reached my full level of womanhood I forced myself to walk on a different path thinking I would end up some place better than I felt she did.

But that didn't happen I had only taken a detour to bring me back to the path God had chosen for me all along. I felt that mama gave up her body freely to men like it was nothing special. But she never wanted me to have sex if it was up to her. Later to find out that she too had been molested. Having sex didn't mean anything to her she didn't have feelings of self-worth. But she knew it keep a man for a while. So she used it as a weapon just as I did.

Once I began writing about my life I began to heal from the inside out. I speak very open with my children about all the things that I had gone through as a young child up until my adulthood so that they would be aware of the things families that people keep hush, hush. Now a 47 year old healed woman my plans are to continue writing in hopes of helping someone overcome some of the same obstacles I had to get over.

I want my readers to keep my family in your prayers, and we will keep you all in ours as well.

Thank you for purchasing this book

Continue to look out for my next project.
Thank you all for your support.

Luv,
Lesia Lipz

THE END